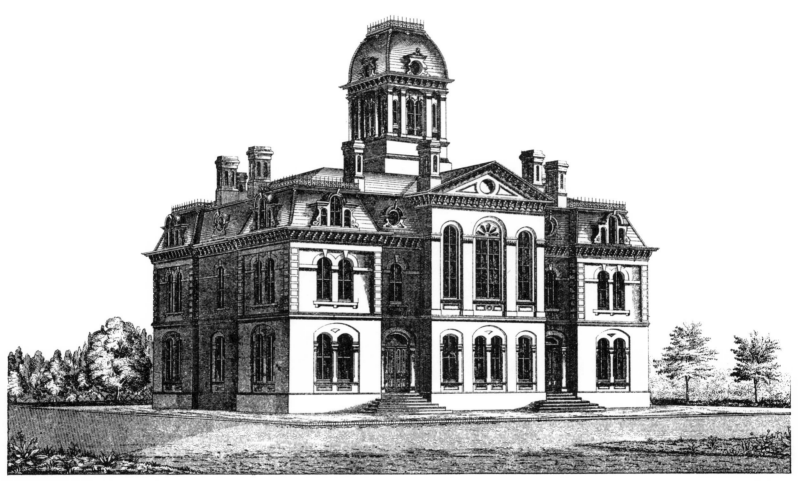

BAY COUNTY COURT HOUSE.
Bay City, Mich.

BICKNELL'S VICTORIAN BUILDINGS

Floor Plans and Elevations for 45 Houses and Other Structures

A. J. BICKNELL & CO.

Dover Publications, Inc.
New York

NOTE

In this reprint edition a number of the plates have been reduced by 10 per cent. These reductions are indicated on the plates themselves, but no adjustments have been made in the original indications of scale and/or size.

FRONTISPIECE

Perspective view of Bay County Court-house, Bay City, Mich. Plates 49, 50 and 51 show the front and side elevations, plans and details.

Published in Canada by General Publishing Company, Ltd., 30 Lesmill Road, Don Mills, Toronto, Ontario.

Published in the United Kingdom by Constable and Company, Ltd.

This Dover edition, first published in 1979 is an unabridged republication of the work originally published by A. J. Bicknell & Co., New York, in 1878 under the title: *Bicknell's Village Builder and Supplement*.

International Standard Book Number: 0-486-23904-7
Library of Congress Catalog Card Number: 79-52830

Manufactured in the United States of America
Dover Publications, Inc.
180 Varick Street
New York, N.Y. 10014

INTRODUCTION

Several years experience in the sale of Architectural Books has taught us, that in bringing out a practical work on Architecture, it is necessary to include a great variety of styles of buildings; and in presenting this volume to the public, we feel assured that it is better adapted to the North, South, East and West, than any previous production of similar character.

Several well-known architects, whose names will be found in connection with the description of plates, have aided us in perfecting this work. It has been our object in the selection of designs principally to include buildings of moderate cost, although we have introduced several elaborate specimens, all of which are suggestive, and may be executed in a plainer way for one-half the given cost.

The estimates are made at the various localities where the designs have been prepared; including Boston, Worcester, Philadelphia, Buffalo, Chicago, St. Louis; Springfield and Lincoln, Ill.; Kansas City, Mo.; Nashville, Tenn.; and Fort Edward, N.Y.

The work is chiefly made up of elevations, plans and details of cottages, villas, and suburban houses; yet much attention has been given to model designs for churches, court-houses, and other public and private buildings.

The elevations are mostly drawn on a scale of one-eighth, one-twelfth, or one-sixteenth; the details on a scale of one-half to three-fourths of one inch to the foot; all of which can be easily comprehended and executed.

The demand for previous publications that we have brought to public notice is an evidence of the increasing want of such a work as the VILLAGE BUILDER , which is not characterized by the style of any one author or locality, but is general in its adaptation.

A. J. BICKNELL & CO.

PREFACE TO THE FIFTH EDITION

In offering this, the fifth edition of the Village Builder, and Supplement, we desire to call attention to the changes made since its original issue. Plate 2 B. has been added, Plates 5 and 6 combined on Plate 5, and a new plate added in place of Plate 6, showing 2 designs of moderate cost. Plate 55 also is an addition, showing designs for inside finish of Stores, Banks and Insurance Offices. We also refer to additional details on Plates 20, 23, 25 and 27. The costs given are the same as in the first editions, although, at the present cost of building materials and labor, many of the designs could now be executed at from 30% to 40% less than estimates here given. With a just appreciation of the generous reception this work has received throughout our own and other countries, we are

Very respectfully,

A. J. BICKNELL & CO.

New York, May 1, 1878.

PLATE 1.

The designs on this plate are drawn on the scale of one-eighth of one inch to the foot.

Fig. 1.

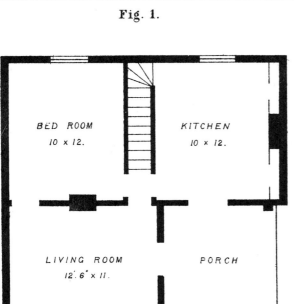

Fig. 2.

| BED ROOM 10 × 12. | KITCHEN 10 × 12. |
| LIVING ROOM 12'. 6" × 11. | PORCH |

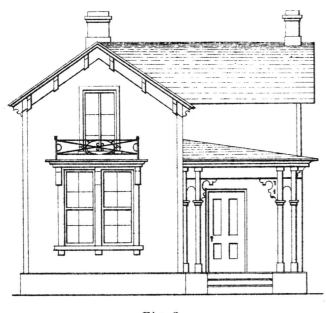

Fig. 3.

Scale: ⅛ of 1 inch to the foot

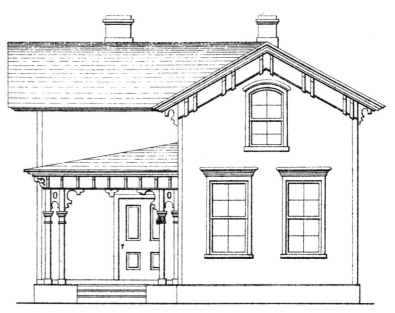

Fig. 4.

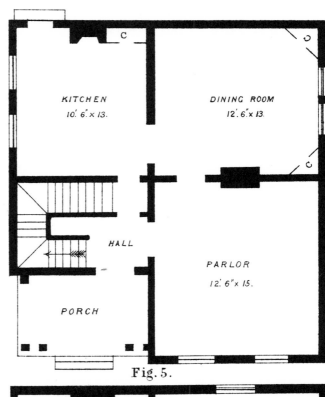

KITCHEN 10'. 6" × 13.	DINING ROOM 12'. 6" × 13.
HALL	PARLOR 12'. 6" × 15.
PORCH	

Fig. 5.

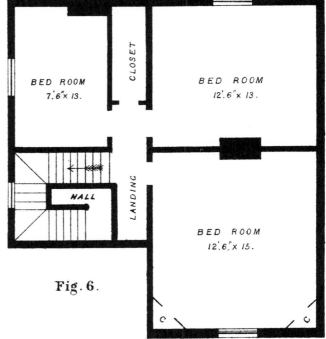

BED ROOM 7'. 6" × 13.	CLOSET	BED ROOM 12'. 6" × 13.
HALL	LANDING	
		BED ROOM 12'. 6" × 15.

Fig. 6.

PLATE 1

PLATE 2.

DESIGN FOR A FRENCH COTTAGE.

LYMAN UNDERWOOD, Architect, 13 Exchange Street, Boston.

The front elevation and floor plans of this cottage are perhaps, sufficiently explicit. It is simply but conveniently arranged for a small family. It is intended to be built of wood, and painted to harmonize with the surroundings. The stories are ten and nine feet. The elevation is drawn to a scale of eight feet to one inch, and the floors sixteen feet to one inch. The cost under ordinary circumstances would be about $3,800.

FRONT ELEVATION.

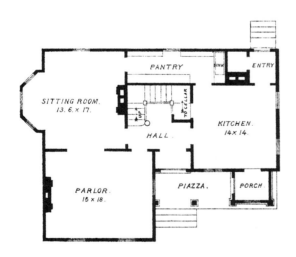

PLAN OF FIRST FLOOR.

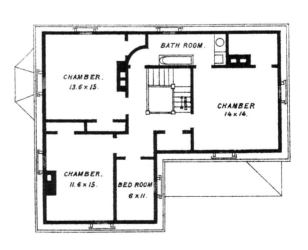

PLAN OF SECOND FLOOR.

PLATE 2

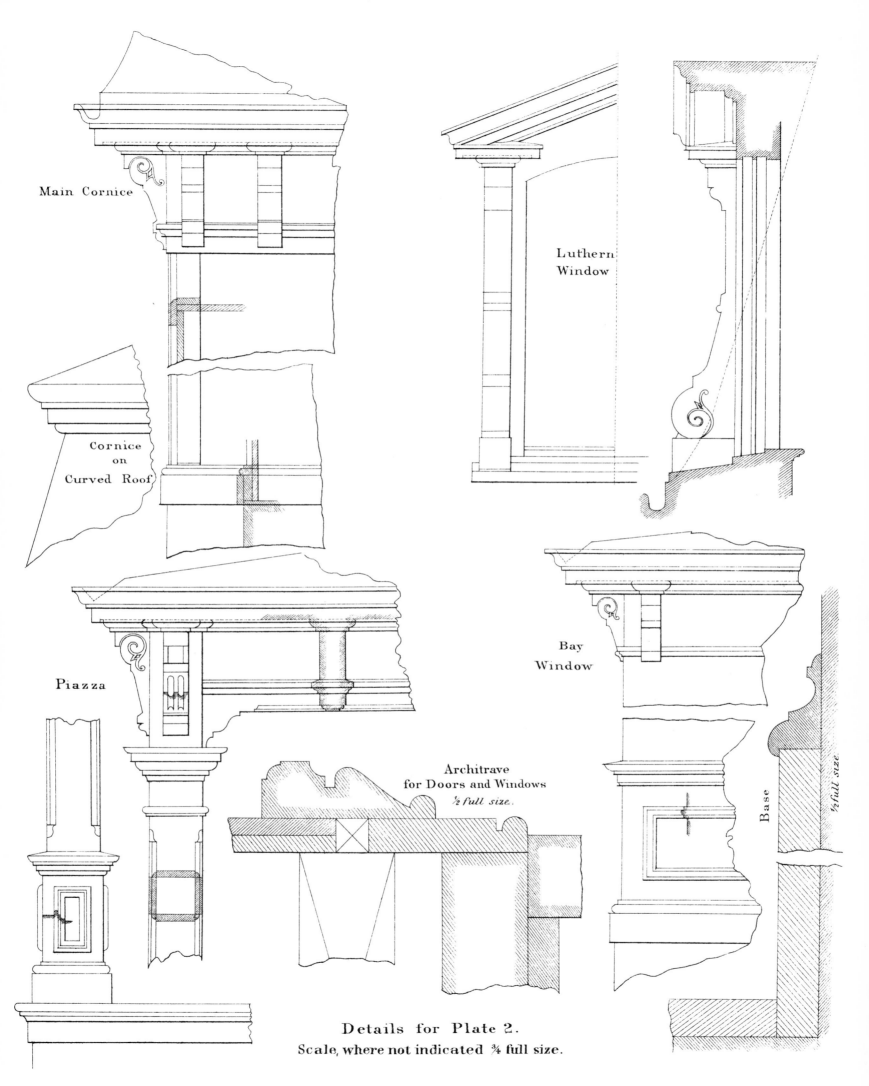

Main Cornice

Cornice
on
Curved Roof

Piazza

Luthern
Window

Bay
Window

Base

½ full size.

Architrave
for Doors and Windows
½ full size.

Details for Plate 2.
Scale, where not indicated ¾ full size.

PLATE 2B

SPECIFICATIONS.

SPECIFICATIONS of the Materials to be Furnished and Labor to be Performed in the Erection and Completion of a Wooden Dwelling-House, according to a set of plans, shown on Plate 2, furnished by L. Underwood, Architect, 13 Exchange Street, Boston.

GENERAL DESCRIPTION.

The size of the house and the size and arrangement of all the rooms, etc., are to be as shown on the plans, which are to be considered as a part of this specification ; and which, with the writing and figures thereon, together with the detail drawings, are to be adhered to in every respect. The figures in all cases are to take the precedence of measurements on the plans.

EXCAVATION, STONE WORK, &c.

The contractor is to do all of the excavating for the cellar, drains and cistern, dig well, etc., and to put in the cellar and bulkhead walls, build foundations for piers and chimneys, and to do all the stonework necessary to receive the frame. The cellar and bulkhead walls are to be 18′ thick at the bottom and 14″ at the top, built with stone laid in cement mortar, and are to be carried up to the proper height to receive the sills. The cellar is to be 8′ 6″ deep in the clear of the joists. There is to be a dry well, 4′ in diameter at the bottom and 2′ 6″ at the top, and 6′ deep, built where shown on the plans. The walls are to be of stone laid dry, carried up to within 18″ of the top of the ground and covered with flagging stones. There is to be a 5″ vitrified earthenware drain-pipe from the waste-pipe to the sink, to the dry well, provided with a stench trap. The cellar wall above the grade is to be built of large stone, with an even face on the outside. The joints are to be well pointed and drawn. There is to be a well located as per plan, and bricked up with a 4″ wall of hard burned brick, laid in cement and is to be covered with flagging stones.

All earth that is excavated is to be deposited in such places in the lot as the proprietor may direct

BRICKWORK.

Piers are to be built, as shown on the cellar plan, with good hard burned brick, and carried up to the sills. The chimneys are to be built, as shown on the plans, of a good quality of chimney brick, and to be topped out with good hard burned brick of uniform color, according to designs given in the elevations. All of the flues are to be fastened throughout on the inside. There are to be funnel irons, of such sizes as may be directed, put in the chimneys, so that stoves may be put up in all the rooms.

There is to be a rain-water cistern, as shown on the plans, of 2,500 gallons capacity, built in the usual manner, with hard burned bricks laid in cement, and is to be thoroughly cemented on the inside, and provided with a flagging stone cover and a vitrified earthen overflow pipe connected with the drain running to the dry well. The overflow pipe is to have a bend-trap.

CARPENTERS' WORK.

The frame is to be made and set up in a good and workmanlike manner, with good, sound, square-edged spruce timbers and joists of such sizes as are marked on the plans. The floor joists are to be bridged with truss bridging. The walls and roof to be boarded with sound pine boards, mill-planed and matched ; to be well laid and nailed. The roofs are to be prepared for slating or tinning, as may be required. The outside finish is to be well wrought and put up according to the detail drawings, and is to be of sound, seasoned pine lumber, free from knots, sap or shakes. The walls of the house are to be clapboarded with Eastern pine clapboards, planed to an even thickness and moulded, and laid so as to lap not less than 1½″, and all to be thoroughly nailed.

All projections, mitre-joints, and other exposed places are to be well leaded with sheet lead so as to prevent all leakage.

SLATING AND TINNING.

All the roofs are to be slated with good Pennsylvania slates of uniform color, laid on tarred sheathing paper, and secured with Swedes iron nails. The slates on the Mansard roofs are to be 8″ × 12″, with the lower ends rounded.

The roofs of the Bay and Luthern windows, and of the piazza, are to be tinned with the best quality of roofing tin, put on with soldered joints. The chimneys and all other places liable to leak are to be secured with lead or zinc and made perfectly tight.

The gutters to the main roof are to be of wood and formed as shown on the details of cornice, and to have lead eaves pipes, and two 3″ (inside measurement) round wooden conductors put up where directed. The gutters for piazza and bay window are also to be of wood, with 2″ wooden conductors. As many of the conductors are to connect with the cistern as may be directed. All others are to have proper turnouts at the bottom.

WINDOWS.

The window-frames are to be made according to the detail drawings, with Southern hard pine, pulley stiles and parting beads. The pockets for the weights are to be cut into the pulley stiles and secured with screws. The sashes are to be of pine 1¾″ thick, and double hung with weights, best hemp sash cord, and 1¼″ axle pulleys, and to be provided with good bronzed sash fastenings. The stop-beads are to be of soft pine, and are to be secured with round-headed blued iron screws.

The cellar windows are to have plank frames made in the usual manner, and the sashes to be hung so as to swing up under the first floor. The glass is to be of such sizes as are figured on the plans.

There are to be outside blinds on all the windows, to be hung with wrought-iron hinges and secured with good substantial fastenings.

PARTITIONS AND FURRINGS.

All partitions are to be set with 2″ × 3″ joists, placed 16″ from centers and bridged. All are to be of even widths, and to be set straight and true. The cappings to the hall partitions are to be 3″ × 4″. All the partition joists, when practicable, are to go through the floor and stand on the partition cap below.

All ceilings are to be furred with 1″ × 3″ strips, placed 16″ between centers, made straight, and all to be well nailed. All necessary grounds are to be put on to fully prepare for plastering. All other places requiring it are to be furred in a proper manner.

LATHING AND PLASTERING.

All the walls and ceilings throughout the house are to be lathed with good pine or spruce laths, assorted so as to be entirely free from knots, in all of the principal rooms. All are to be plastered with a heavy coat of lime and hair mortar evenly floated, and skim-coated with beach sand finish. All angles are to be made straight and true.

There are to be stucco cornices and centerpieces in the front hall, parlor, and sitting-room. The cornices to cost, on an average, 37 cents per foot, and the centerpieces to cost, in the aggregate, $25.

INSIDE FINISH.

The inside finish is to be of clear and thoroughly kiln-dried pine lumber. The style of finish is to be as shown on detail drawings and put up in a thorough and workmanlike manner. There is to be a moulded base in all of the principal rooms throughout the house. All of the clothes closets are to have shelves and drawers as marked on the plans, and to have two strips on all sides where there are no drawers or shelves and provided with hooks screwed on not over 8″ apart. The store room and china closet are to be finished with drawers and shelves. The sink is to be finished with a closet underneath. The under floors are to be of good, sound, seasoned square-edged pine or spruce mill-planed boards, laid edge to edge. The upper floors are to be of narrow widths of seasoned pine, mill-planed, jointed, well laid and smoothed off. All floors are to be cut in between the bases.

The bath-tub, water-closet and wash-stand in the bath-room are to be finished with black walnut. The water-closet seat and the tub are to be paneled and moulded. The wash-bowl case is to be finished with drawers and a closet underneath. There is to be a paper box in the water-closet seat.

The front outside doors are to be double and of the sizes marked on the plan, to be 1¾" thick and to have raised mouldings. The upper panels are to be of glass. The rear outside door is to be of such size as marked on the plan 1¾" thick and moulded with raised mouldings. All other doors throughout the house are to be 1½" thick and moulded with raised mouldings. All doors are to be of such sizes as are figured on the plans and to have glass panels where marked.

All doors are to be of the best quality of kiln-dried pine lumber.

STAIRS.

The stairs are to be located and built as shown on the plans. They are to be finished with good clear pine lumber and to have a 7" (shaft measurement) chamfered newel post, 4" moulded rail and 1¾" fancy turned balusters, all to be of thoroughly seasoned black walnut. The landing and gallery posts are to be 5" and chamfered.

The cellar stairs are to be built in a good and substantial manner.

Build and set up the steps to front and back doors with good, sound, seasoned 2" hard pine plank. The front steps to have a moulding under the treads with returned nosings.

HARDWARE.

All doors are to be hung with good loose-jointed butts of suitable sizes for their respective places, and to have brass bolt mortise locks with brass plate and keys, and all to have pressed glass knobs and bronzed trimmings. The front doors to be trimmed with flush bolts and to have a lock with night-latch and furnished with duplicate keys. The knobs on the outside to be silvered glass with silver-plated trimmings. The knob inside is to be of pressed glass.

The front door is to be provided with a bell hung in such place as may be directed. The pull is to be of silvered glass and to correspond with the front door knobs.

GAS PIPES.

Gas pipes are to be put into the ceiling of the parlor, sitting room, front hall and kitchen, and in all other rooms where marked on the plans.

PLUMBING.

There is to be a 2' × 4' cast-iron sink at the end of the pantry to be furnished with a 1½" waste-pipe, cesspool strainer, etc., to make the same complete.

There is to be a 3" copper pump at the sink to be provided with a 1½" bore, 2½ lb. lead pipe to connect with the well.

There is to be a 2½" force pump of the best quality, provided with a two ways faucet and 1½" galvanized iron suction pipe connecting with the rain water cistern.

The rising main connecting with the cistern in the bath-room is to be 1¼" in diameter, 2½ lbs. per foot.

The bath-room is to be fitted up with bath-tub, water-closet and wash-bowl. The bath-tub is to be of the usual size, lined with planished copper and furnished with a ⅝" brass faucet, plug, chain, and rose overflow.

The water-closet is to be the best pan closet with wedgwood basin, strong lead trap and 4" iron soil pipe and is to be provided with all necessary pipes, service boxes, and other fixtures to make the same complete in every respect.

The wash-bowl is to be 15" of marbled pattern, to have a countersunk marble top 1" thick with moulded edge and to have 8" marble back and ends. The faucet, chain, holder and plug are to be silver-plated. The wash-bowl case is to be lined up underneath with lead 4″ high and to have a suitable sized waste pipe connecting with the soil pipe.

There is to be a cistern over the bath-room of 300 gallons capacity, lined with 5 lb. sheet lead and to be provided with all the necessary pipes, valves, etc., to make the same complete in every respect.

The supply pipe for the bath-tub is to be $\frac{3}{4}$″ bore, $2\frac{1}{2}$ lbs. per foot, for wash-bowl $\frac{5}{8}$″ bore, $1\frac{1}{2}$ lbs. per foot. The waste pipes for tub and bowl are to be $1\frac{1}{2}$″ bore 3 lbs. per foot. All materials of good quality necessary to complete the plumber's work in every respect are to furnished and all the work is to be done in a good and workmanlike manner.

PAINTING AND GLAZING.

All of the woodwork outside and inside that is usually painted, is to have three good coats of paint of the best quality all to be tinted as may be directed. The closet floors are to be painted. All gutters and tinned roofs are to be painted with three good coats of paint. The blinds are to be painted four coats of such color as may be directed. The stair rails and all hard woodwork are to be filled and well rubbed down in oil. All hard pine work is to be puttied and well oiled.

All of the sashes are to be glazed with the best German glass, all to be well bedded, bradded and back puttied. The front doors are to be glazed with ground glass of such pattern as may be selected. All other glass panel doors are to have plain ground glass.

FINALLY.

It is to be understood that everything necessary to the full and complete execution of the work according to the general intent and meaning of these plans and specifications is to be done and all materials furnished so as to complete the work in a good and workmanlike manner whether herein particularly described or not.

FORM OF CONTRACT

FOR THE BUILDING OF DESIGN SHOWN ON PLATE TWO.

Memorandum of agreement made between A. B., of ———, in the County of ———, and Commonwealth of ———, of the first part, and C. D., of ———, in the county and commonwealth aforesaid, builder, of the second part, touching the erection of a wooden dwelling house for said A. B., to be located on ——— street, in ———, and to completely finish the same in all its parts by the party of the second part, according to the full intent and meaning of the plans and specifications of even date herewith and signed by both parties hereto, said plans and specifications to be considered as a part of this agreement.

The said C. D., in consideration of the covenants and agreements hereinafter contained by the said A. B. to be kept and performed, does covenant, promise and agree that he the said C. D. shall commence the work immediately and prosecute it to its completion without any delays of the same, except such as are inevitably caused by the strike of workmen or the state of the weather, and that he will perform all labor and furnish all materials necessary to complete the work so as to satisfy the provisions of this contract in accordance with the requirements of the plans and specifications in the most thorough and workmanlike manner under the superintendence of

to his satisfaction and to the acceptance of the owner on or before the ——— day of ——— now next ensuing the date hereof. And it is hereby expressly agreed that the said C. D. shall pay and allow the said A. B. for each and every day (except the aforesaid) beyond said ——— of ——— the sum of ten dollars as liquidate damages. But if the work is delayed by causes aforesaid, the said C. D. is to be allowed one extra day for each and every day of delay to complete said work.

And the said A. B. in consideration of the above premises doth for himself and his executors agree well and truly to pay or cause to be paid unto the said C. D. or his legal representatives the following sum to wit : Three thousand eight hundred dollars in the manner following, that is to say, when the cellar is finished and the building raised and boarded, one thousand dollars : when the outside is completed one thousand dollars : when the plastering is finished eight hundred dollars, and the balance one thousand dollars in thirty days after the building is completed and accepted by the architect and proprietor free from all charges by way of lien or other attachments.

No extra work shall be performed or materials furnished beyond that provided for by this agreement and the plans and specifications aforesaid, nor shall the work be changed or in anywise varied by the said C. D., except upon request made by the said A. B., who shall have the right to vary and alter so far as respects any part of the work or materials at any time remaining to be performed or finished by the said C. D. And in case a request is made by said A. B. to have any change or alterations made, the price shall be agreed upon and the bargain made in writing and signed by both parties hereto before such changes or alterations are commenced. And if any difference of opinion shall arise in regard to the price of extra work, it shall be referred to the architect and two disinterested persons, one to be chosen by each of the parties hereto and whose decision shall be final and binding upon all parties.

It is further agreed that insurance shall be effected upon the building in some company approved by the said A. B., immediately after the first payments to the amount of that payment, and to be increased after each payment to the amount of the sum of all the payments then made. Said policy of insurance is to be in the name and for the benefit of said A. B. in case of loss, he paying one half and the said C. D. paying one half the expense of the policy.

In witness whereof the said parties of the first and second parts have hereunto set their hands and seals this ——— day of ——— one thousand eight hundred and

Executed in presence of

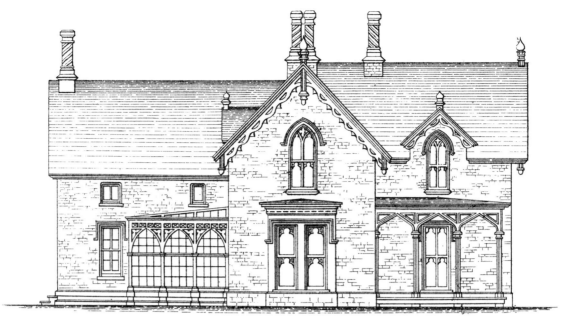

SIDE ELEVATION.

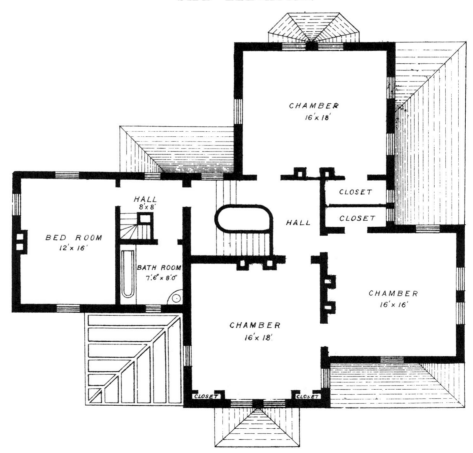

2ᴰ STORY PLAN.

PLATE 4

SPECIFICATIONS.

SPECIFICATIONS of the Materials to be Furnished and Labor to be Performed in the Erection and Completion of a one and a half story Cottage, in the Gothic style, for Mr. ——, in the City of St. Louis, State of Missouri. (See Plates Three and Four for the elevations and plans.)

GENERAL DESCRIPTION.

The building will have a frontage on Lafayette Avenue of forty-three feet, by a depth of fifty feet, there will be a cellar under the entire building 7′ 6″ deep, the first story will be 11′ high, the second story will be 10′ high to underside of cellar beams; all these heights to be in the clear when finished. For position of doors and windows and arrangement of rooms reference is hereby had to plans.

EXCAVATION.

The earth to be dug out the proper depth and extent to receive the cellar and foundation walls, dig trenches for footing courses under all walls two feet wide and six inches deep; all earth not required to fill in around walls and to grade lot to be carted away. The cellar to be dug 5′ below the grade of lot, cesspool to be 7′ diameter and 15′ deep.

RUBBLE STONE WORK.

All the cellar and foundation walls are to be built up straight and plumb to the under side of sill eighteen inches thick, the footings six inches deep and two feet wide; the work to be of the best quality of quarry building limestone, laid up with fresh lime and sharp sand mortar, and all joints well pointed, and the work well bonded with through stone, the top course to be of broad flat rock not less than three feet thick, the outside of walls where exposed to be tuck pointed.

TIMBER WORK.

All timber used throughout to be of a sound quality and as well seasoned as can be procured, and of the following dimensions:—The sills to be 4″ × 6″; the first and second tier of joist to be 2″ × 10″, properly framed and placed 16″ from centers; the second tier of joist will be notched on a 1″ × 6″ ribbon piece let in the side studding; the collar beams will be 2″ × 6″ spiked to side of rafters; the wall plate will be 2″ × 4″ spiked to top of studding; the studding will be 2″ × 6″ placed 16″ from centers; the corner posts will be 4″ × 6″ framed in sill; the braces 3″ × 4″ framed in corner posts and sill, draw bored and pinned; the rafters 2″ × 6″ properly framed and well secured to wall plate, and placed 16″ from centers, secured at the top to 2″ × 8″ ridge piece. Each tier of joist will have one row of cross bridging through the center of 1½″ × 2″, well nailed to joist, the perch timbers will be 2″ × 6″ properly framed and put up as shown.

SIDING.

The building enclosed with second rate dressed white pine weather boarding and to have 1¼″ lap at joints.

ROOFING.

The roof will be sheathed with 1″ sheathing boards, and covered with the best quality of white pine sawed shingles laid 4½″ to the weather with the joints well broken.

FLOORING.

The floors will be laid with the best second-rate white pine mill-worked flooring, well seasoned and laid in courses of not over 5½″ wide, well nailed to each joist and cleaned off, when finished; the perch floors will be laid in courses of not over 3½″ wide, with white lead in the joints.

CORNICES.

Prepare and put eave gable and porch cornices as shown, of good well-seasoned white pine free from sap or large knots ; prepare gutter beds for metal gutters, as shown.

PLASTERING.

All the rooms to be lathed with pine laths, and to have two coats of brown mortar, and skim with plaster paris—finish well with trowel ; all angles to be made straight and plumb.

WINDOWS.

All the windows throughout to have double hung box frames, the sash $1\frac{3}{4}''$ thick and made as shown, the sizes as shown on elevation, and hung with $1\frac{3}{4}$ axle pulleys and patent sash cord ; each window to have sash locks to cost $ per dozen. All the windows throughout will be provided with outside rolling slat blinds, $1\frac{3}{8}''$ thick, hung with patent spiral blind hinges, and well fastened. The cellar windows will have solid $2''$ plank frames, with $1\frac{3}{8}''$ sash made in two parts, and hung with loose butts and fastened with good bolts ; the exterior finish of frames will be as shown.

BAY WINDOWS.

To be constructed as shown on plan ; the roofs will be covered with the best roofing tin, painted on the under sides.

PORCHES.

Put up as shown on drawings, of good sound white pine lumber, well seasoned ; the under side of roof ceiled with matched boards, smoothed and beaded ; the roofs will be covered the same as bay windows. The steps will be made of $1\frac{1}{4}'$ white pine.

CONSERVATORY.

Built as shown on plan and elevation ; the sashes of sides made $1\frac{3}{4}''$ thick, and hung on pivots in center of sides ; the roof will be of glass, properly set in sky-light sash, and arranged for proper ventilation.

TIN WORK.

Put in eave gutters of one cross leaded tin $14''$ wide, well painted on both sides ; put up down spouts, $3\frac{1}{2}''$ diameter, at the several points where required, with proper elbows.

INTERIOR FINISH.

The inside finish will be of good second-rate white pine, well seasoned ; the rooms and hall of main building, first story, will be finished with a neat moulded casing $8''$ wide, and $11''$ moulded base ; the second story will have plain $6''$ moulded casing, $7''$ moulded base ; the kitchen, servants' and bath-rooms finished with a plain $5''$ casing, and $6''$ beaded base ; the windows of main house will have moulded panel backs, the others finished to stool and apron pieces.

DOORS.

All doors throughout will be made in four panels and moulded on both sides. Those on first story will be $3' \times 7'\,6''$, $1\frac{3}{4}''$ thick ; those in the second story, $2'\,10'' \times 6'\,10''$; the closet doors will be as large as the spaces will properly admit ; the front door will be made the same style as shown, there will be raised mouldings on the outside. All doors to be hung to $2''$ rabbeted frames, with proper butts, and to have hard wood carpet strips. The locks in the first story will be $5''$ mortise, with white and silver-plated trimming ; all others will have $5''$ tumbler rim locks, with brown knobs and bronze trimming ; the outside doors to be secured with suitable bolts.

PAINTING.

All wood and other work usually painted to have three good coats of lead and oil paint of any color the owner may desire. All interior finish of doors and windows, with the door, frames inside of sash and base, will be grained in oak, neat style and varnished ; the blinds painted Paris green.

GLAZING.

All windows to be glazed with the best quality of Pittsburgh glass, well tinned, bedded, and back puttied.

MANTLES.

The three principal rooms of the first story will be provided with marble mantles, to cost $75 each ; those in the second story to have a neat wooden mantle, to cost $12 each.

GRATES.

The grates of first story to cost $14 each, those in second story $12 each—to be three in each story—these prices to be exclusive of the setting; they are to be set with fire brick in the best manner.

CHIMNEYS.

Are to be built of good brick, as shown ; the flues to be $9'' \times 12''$, well pargeted on the inside work in a $6''$ thimble in kitchen flue ; the chimneys topped out with best quality of red brick and surmounted with chimney tops of terra cotta.

GAS PIPES.

To be run through the building so as to furnish light for each room and halls, the outlets will be placed where the owner may desire, the pipes to be the sizes required by gas companies' regulations.

BELLS.

There will be two bells in the building—one to front door, and one in parlor.

STAIRS.

The stairs will be built on strong carriages. The main stairs will be of clear yellow pine, $1''$ thick for the treads, and $\frac{7}{8}''$ white pine risers, finished with return nosing scotia and fillets ; the rail will be $2\frac{1}{8}''$ thick, $4\frac{1}{4}''$ wide moulded ; the balusters will be $1\frac{3}{4}''$ fancy turned base and neck ; the newell will be $10''$, with turned base and cap, and octagon panel shaft ; and all to be of well seasoned black walnut. The steps and risers will be housed in the wall-string, the stairs will be enclosed underneath with a panelled and moulded spandrill ; the rear steps will be of yellow pine and white pine risers, finished with plain turned balusters and $2'' \times 3''$ walnut hand rail ; $7''$ turned newell post, of black walnut. Those stairs will be enclosed underneath with matched ceiling boards, smoothed and beaded, with a door leading to cellar by a strong stairway with plain rail.

PLUMBERS' WORK.

There will be a $6'$ copper planished bath-tub, fitted up in bath-room, with all the necessary supply, and waste-pipe and compression draw-cocks for hot and cold water ; also fitted up in kitchen, a 40 gallon copper boiler, with all necessary pipe to connect to bath-tub, sink and wash-basin ; also put up in bath-room, a marble top wash-basin with supply and waste-pipe, and draw-cocks of an approved kind ; and also fit up an iron sink in the kitchen, with supply-pipe for hot and cold water, and $1\frac{1}{2}''$ waste-pipe. All supply-pipe will be extra strong $\frac{5}{8}''$; the waste water from bath-room and kitchen will be conducted to sewer running through the cellar ; the sewer will be of $12''$ stone drain-pipe, and will be continued from the cellar to cesspool in yard.

CLOSETS.

The closets will be fitted up with shelves, strips, and clothes hooks as desired ; the store-rooms and china closet will be shelved as may be required ; close up under sink and hang small door and fasten with spring catch.

CONDITIONS.

That all material and labor used are to be the best of their respective kinds, and if there is anything omitted in these specifications, or that is not fully shown on the plans, which should be necessary for the full completion of the building, according to the full intent and meaning of these specifications and accompanying drawings, the same is to be done at the expense of the contractor without extra charge ; and, in case of any alteration, addition, or deduction, the price shall be agreed upon in writing before going into effect ; and no extras will be allowed unless first agreed upon, and the price fixed. The work to be under the superintendence of Alfred Grable, architect, who will have power to reject any material or labor which, in his opinion, is not in accordance with these specifications.

APPROVED FORM OF CONTRACT

ADOPTED BY THE ST. LOUIS CO-OPERATIVE BUILDING ASSOCIATION.

ARTICLES OF AGREEMENT, made and entered into this   day of   Eighteen hundred and sixty eight, by and between the SAMUEL P. SIMPSON party of the First part, and Messrs. BROWN AND GRABLE with D. T. WRIGHT, as security party of the Second part, all of the city and county of St. Louis, State of Missouri, in the words and figures as follows:

The said party of the Second part, covenant and agree to and with the said party of the First part, to make and erect, build and finish a certain two story brick dwelling house on a certain lot of ground, situated on McPherson Avenue, between Warne and Sarah Avenues, for SAMUEL P. SIMPSON, Esq., in accordance with the drawings, plans and elevations, and specifications furnished by the superintending architect, and adopted for said buildings, which are hereto annexed and made a part of this contract.

The said party of the Second part, shall at their own cost and charges, provide and deliver all and every kind of material of good and sound quality and description, together with the cartage, scaffolding, tackles, tools, templets, rules, moulds, matters and things, labor and work, which may be necessary for the due, proper and complete execution of this contract, and accordingly erect, build, finish and complete in a good, sound, workmanlike manner to the perfect satisfaction and approbation of the superintendent, J. H. McCLAREN Esq., the aforesaid buildings and works, according to the specifications, drawings, dimensions and explanations and observations thereon, or herein stated, described or implied or incident thereto, which may become necessary to the true intent and meaning thereof, although not specially and specifically stated or described by the aforesaid drawings and specifications.

And should it appear, that any of the works hereby intended to be done, or matters relative thereto are not fully detailed or explained in the said specifications and drawings, the said party of the Second part shall apply to the superintendent for such further detailed explanations, and perform his orders as part of this contract.

The superintendent shall be at liberty to make any deviation from or alteration in the plan, form, construction, detail and execution, described by the drawings and specifications, without invaliding or rendering void this contract, and in case of any difference in the expense, an addition to or abatement from the contract price shall be made, and the same shall be determined by the architect.

And the said superintendent shall have full power and lawful authority to reject the whole or any part or portion of said materials or work, which may not in his opinion be in strict accordance with the letter and spirit of these presents; and if by reason of any act or deed on the part of the said party of the Second part, the said party of the First part, or its legal representatives, or the superintendent, shall be led to believe that the erection or completion of said buildings is retarded unnecessarily, they or either of them may, as often as the same appears to them necessary, furnish such works and materials as they may deem necessary to facilitate the completion of said buildings, and the cost and expense thereof is to be borne by and chargeable to the party of the Second part exclusively.

And in case of any alteration or change that may be directed by the said superintendent as aforesaid in the plans, drawings and construction of the aforesaid buildings, and in case of any omission or addition to said buildings being required by said superintendent, the cost and expense thereof is to be agreed upon in writing, and such agreement is to be signed by said party of the Second part and superintendent before the same is done, or before any allowance therefor can be claimed; and in case of any failure so to agree, the same shall be completed upon the original plan

And in case of frost or inclemency of weather, the said party of the Second part shall effectually cover, protect and secure the several works, as occasion may require, and prevent admission of wet through the apertures, and all damages occasioned thereby or otherwise, during the progress of the works and by depredation or fire, the same to be borne and reinstated by and at the expense of the said party of the Second part who shall also case effectually with boarding all bases, capitals, cornices and other projections, and deliver up the building in the most perfect order and condition, fit for use and occupation.

The said St. Louis Co-operative Building Association reserves to itself the right to insure said buildings, during the progress of the works at the costs and expenses of the said party of the Second part.

The work of erecting and finishing said buildings, including all alterations and additions in said contract provided or hereafter agreed upon, is to be proceeded with, with all reasonable dispatch, and the same shall be completed and delivered up to said party of the first part in perfect order and condition, fit for use and occupation on or before the first day of May, of the year Eighteen hundred and sixty-nine, it being agreed that the said party of the Second part shall forfeit the sum of ten dollars for every day expiring after that day, before the completion and delivery of said buildings as aforesaid to the said party of the First part, and this condition not to be made or rendered void by any alteration or additional works being performed, but in such case the time shall be extended as shall be deemed proper by the superintendent and agreed to by the said party of the Second part, at the time of such extension.

The superintendent's opinion, certificate report, and decision on all matters to be binding and conclusive on the party of the Second part.

The said party of the First part agrees and binds itself for and in consideration of the erection of said buildings as aforesaid to pay unto the party of the Second part the sum of seven thousand two hundred and sixty dollars ($7,260).

Payments to be made as the work progresses to the amount of the value of sixty per cent. of the work done, as the superintendent shall estimate it, and 20 per cent. of the contract amount at the completion and delivery of the work, and the residue of 20 per cent., or the balance of the contract price six months after the buildings are completed, and delivered up to the said party of the First part, but the said party of the first part shall have the right at any time after said buildings are completed to settle with and pay said party of the Second part, either in cash or by notes, as may be agreed upon by both parties. It being, however, understood that nothing herein contained shall be in any way so construed as to require the deferred payment to be made in less than six months after the completion and acceptance of the buildings by the party of the First part.

The portion of the contract price contemplated to be paid during the progress of the work, to be paid in instalments and dates as follows, provided that at such dates the progress of the work has made such payments due :—Eight hundred ($800) dollars when the first floor joist is on, eight hundred ($800) dollars when the second floor joist is on, eight hundred ($800) dollars when the roof is on, eight hundred and sixty ($860) dollars when the building is plastered, one thousand ($1,000) dollars when the finish and trimmings are up, fifteen hundred ($1,500) dollars when the building is completed, and the balance as hereinbefore provided for.

Provided, that the wages of artisans and laborers, and all those employed by, or furnishing materials to the said party of the Second part, shall have been paid and satisfied, so that they shall have no lien upon the buildings or works, and in case the said party of the Second part shall fail so to pay and satisfy all and every claim and demand against said buildings as aforesaid, the said party of the First part may, if it deems proper so to do, retain from the moneys due and coming to said party of the Second part, enough to pay and satisfy such claims and demands, it being, however, understood that nothing herein contained shall in any way be construed as impairing the right of the said party of the First part to hold the said party of the Second part, or securities liable on their bond for any breach of the conditions of the same.

Sub-contractors and parties furnishing materials on account of this contract are to be paid by the party of the First part, pro rata, as above stated, upon order from the party of the Second part, and all such payments to be charged to account of this contract.

All payments by the party of the First part to the party of the Second part, or to their orders to be made upon orders from the said superintendent.

In Witness Whereof, we, the several parties to the above contract, have set our hands and seals, the day and year first above written.

WITNESS.   BROWN & GRABLE.   [Seal]

JAMES H. McCLAREN.   D. T. WRIGHT.   [Seal]

P. S.—The above is a copy of contract for the building of a house for Gen'l. Samuel P. Simpson, designed by Alfred Grable, Architect, 416 Locust St., St. Louis, Mo.

PLATE 5.

DESIGN FOR ITALIAN COTTAGE.

E. R. Francisco, Architect, Kansas City, Mo.

Plate 5. Shows the front and side elevations and plans.

Scale of elevations—one-eighth inch to the foot.

Scale of plans---three-thirty-second of an inch to the foot.   Cost, built of wood, $2,000.   Brick, $2,500.

PLATE 6.

C. Edward Loth, Architect, Troy, N.Y.

Fig. 1. Front elevation of one-story frame cottage.   Cost, $1,600.

Fig. 2. Side elevation.

Fig. 3. First floor plan.

Fig. 4. Front elevation of two-story frame house.   Cost, $2,250.

Fig. 5. First floor plan.

Fig. 6. Second floor plan.

The designs on this plate are drawn to scale of three-thirty-second of an inch to the foot.

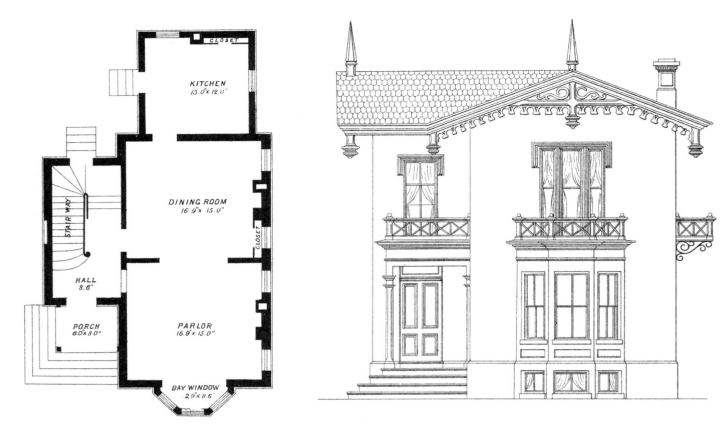

FIRST STORY Scale ³/₃₂ in.

FRONT ELEVATION Scale ⅛ in.

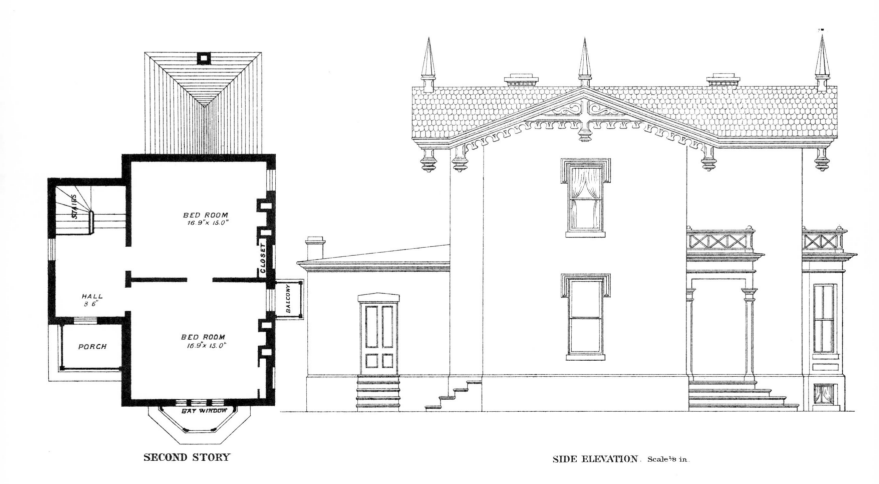

SECOND STORY

SIDE ELEVATION Scale ⅛ in.

PLATE 5   [plate reduced 10 per cent in this reprint edition]

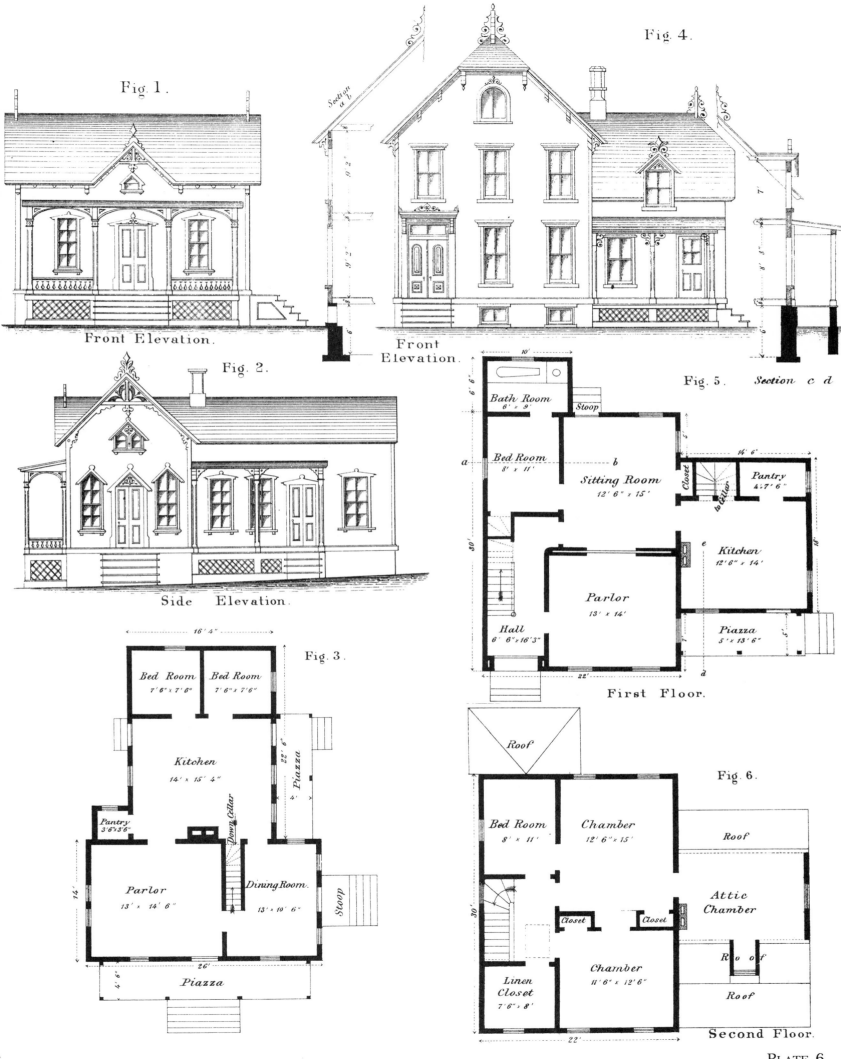

Fig. 1.

Front Elevation.

Fig. 2.

Side Elevation.

Fig. 3.

Bed Room
7' 6" x 7' 6"

Bed Room
7' 6" x 7' 6"

16' 4"

22' 6"

Kitchen
14' x 15' 4"

Piazza

4'

Pantry
3' 6" x 3' 6"

Down Cellar

14'

Parlor
13' x 14' 6"

Dining Room.
13' x 10' 6"

Stoop

26'

4' 6"

Piazza

Fig. 4.

Section a b

9' 2"

9' 2"

8'

6'

Front
Elevation.

Fig. 5.

Section c d

7'

8' 3"

6'

10'

6' 6"

Bath Room
6' x 9'

Stoop

a

30'

Bed Room
8' x 11'

b

Sitting Room
12' 6" x 15'

Closet

to Cellar

14' 6'

Pantry
4' x 7' 6"

18'

Hall
6' 6" x 16' 3"

Parlor
13' x 14'

e

Kitchen
12' 6" x 14'

Piazza
5' x 13' 6"

5'

7'

22'

d

First Floor.

Fig. 6.

Roof

Bed Room
8' x 11'

Chamber
12' 6" x 15'

Roof

30'

Attic
Chamber

Closet

Closet

Linen
Closet
7' 6" x 8'

Chamber
11' 6" x 12' 6"

Roof

Roof

22'

Second Floor.

PLATE 6

PLATES 7, 8, 9.

ELEVATIONS, PLANS AND DETAILS FOR A GOTHIC COTTAGE.

EDGAR BERRYMAN, Architect, 388 Main Street, Buffalo.

Plate 7. Fig. 1 is the front elevation; Fig. 2 A, Vestibule; B, Hall eight feet wide containing main stairs and recess (a) for hat rack; C, Parlor fifteen by eighteen feet; D, Dining-room sixteen by nineteen feet; E, Bed or Sitting-room having large closet H, and Bath-room G, in connection; F, Kitchen; I, Closet; K, Pantry; L, Serving and China Closet; W, rear platform; N, Verandah; height main part eleven feet, rear nine feet four inches.

Plate 8. Fig. 3 side elevation; Fig. 4 V, Platform on level of second floor of rear part; U and T, Bed-rooms; X, Closets; Q, R, S, Chambers; P, Tower containing stairs to Observatory; O, Hall containing niche for Statuary. All on Plates 7 and 8 are drawn twelve feet to an inch.

Plate 9. Contains principal details; A, Tower and gable windows; B, Railing and cornice of Observatory; C, Elevation and section of cornice and butments on Bay windows; D, Main cornice; E, Finial; F, Verandah; G, Chimney tops; L, Stair-case. All one-half inch to the foot. H, O, N, Section of Doors; M and I, Inside finish; K, section of window frame; P, Bases; S, Window-sill; I, Water-table all one and one-half inch to the foot; Q, Plaster cornice and panel moulding; R, Plaster arch over Bay windows and in Hall.

Fig. I.

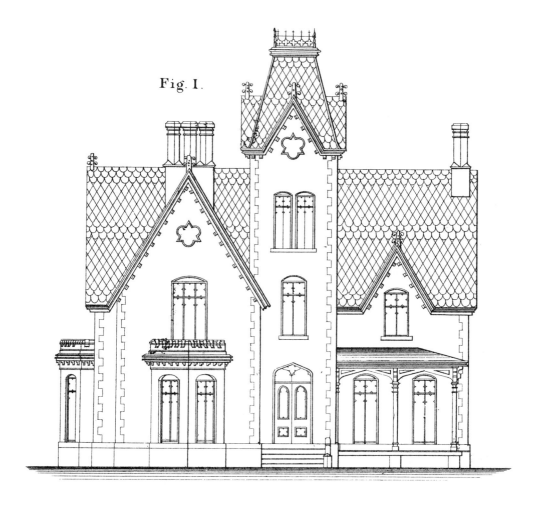

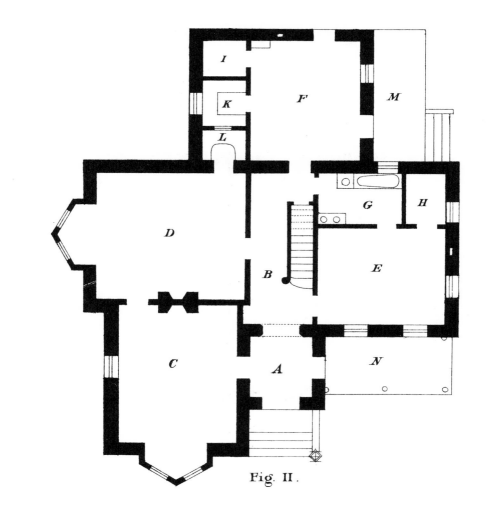

Fig. II.

PLATE 7

Fig. III.

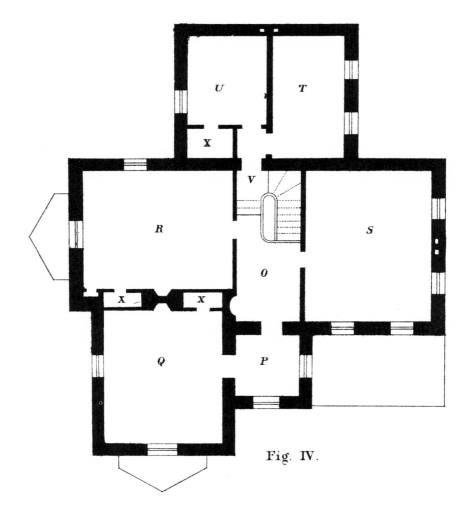

Fig. IV.

PLATE 8

A

B.

C

E

D

O

H

N

M

I

G

F

a

K

P

T

L

S

R

Q

PLATE 9

PLATES 10, 11, 12.

DESIGN FOR A FRAME COTTAGE VILLA.

A. C. BRUCE, Architect, Nashville, Tenn.

Plate 10. Shows the front elevation and first floor plan of a dwelling recently erected for Col. A. S. Colyer, President of the Sawannee Coal Mines. The arrangement has been made without regard to space. All the rooms are large and well ventilated. The doors to the Library and the one on the Parlor entering on the front porch are two folds with sash. The inside doors first story, are three by seven feet with transom over each and moulded on both sides. The front door is of black walnut; the sliding doors are also made of black walnut two and one-half inches thick, moulded below, with ornamental glass panels above. The windows are all double box hung with weights. The first story was plastered to ground when the finish, shown in detail C, was put on, out of first-class yellow pine oiled and varnished. The first story is twelve feet in clear. The plan on the plate is drawn to a scale of three thirty-second of one inch to the foot. The second story is finished with Poplar in a plain manner and neatly painted.

Plate 11. Side elevation and second story plan. Scale three thirty-second of one inch to the foot.

Plate 12. Details of Gable, Front Window, Vestibule and Finial at one-half of one inch to the foot. Section of Architrave at one and one-half inch. Cost $7,500.

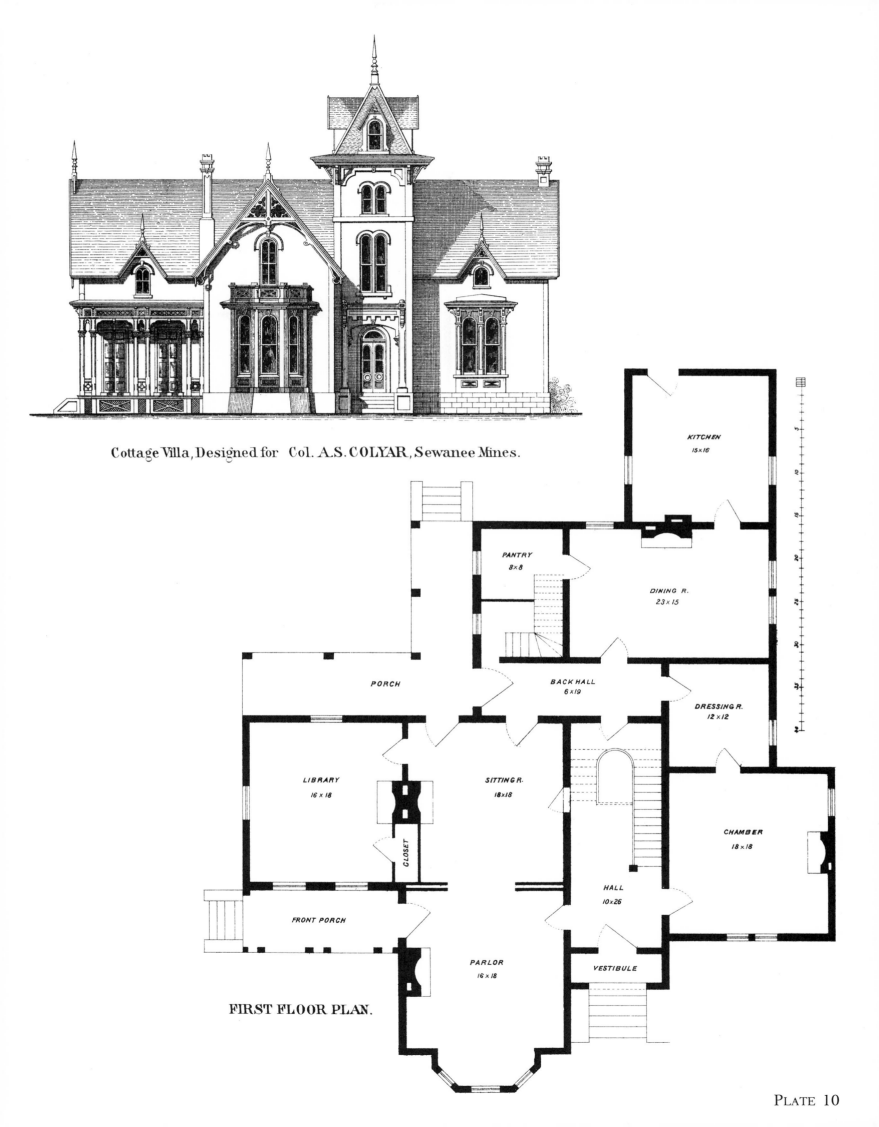

Cottage Villa, Designed for Col. A.S. COLYAR, Sewanee Mines.

KITCHEN
15 × 16

PANTRY
8 × 8

DINING R.
23 × 15

PORCH

BACK HALL
6 × 19

DRESSING R.
12 × 12

LIBRARY
16 × 18

SITTING R.
18 × 18

CLOSET

CHAMBER
18 × 18

FRONT PORCH

HALL
10 × 26

PARLOR
16 × 18

VESTIBULE

FIRST FLOOR PLAN.

PLATE 10

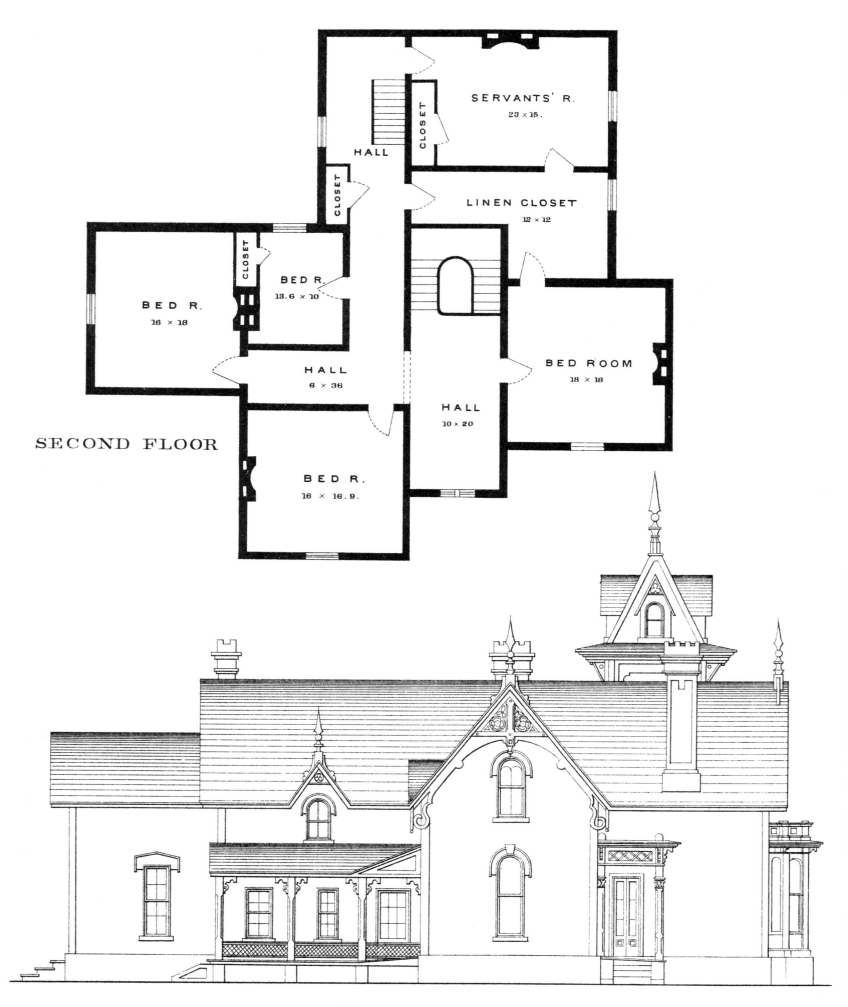

SERVANTS' R.
23 × 15.

CLOSET

HALL

CLOSET

LINEN CLOSET
12 × 12

CLOSET

BED R.
16 × 18

BED R.
13.6 × 10

BED ROOM
18 × 18

SECOND FLOOR

HALL
6 × 36

HALL
10 × 20

HALL

BED R.
16 × 16.9.

SIDE ELEVATION

PLATE 11

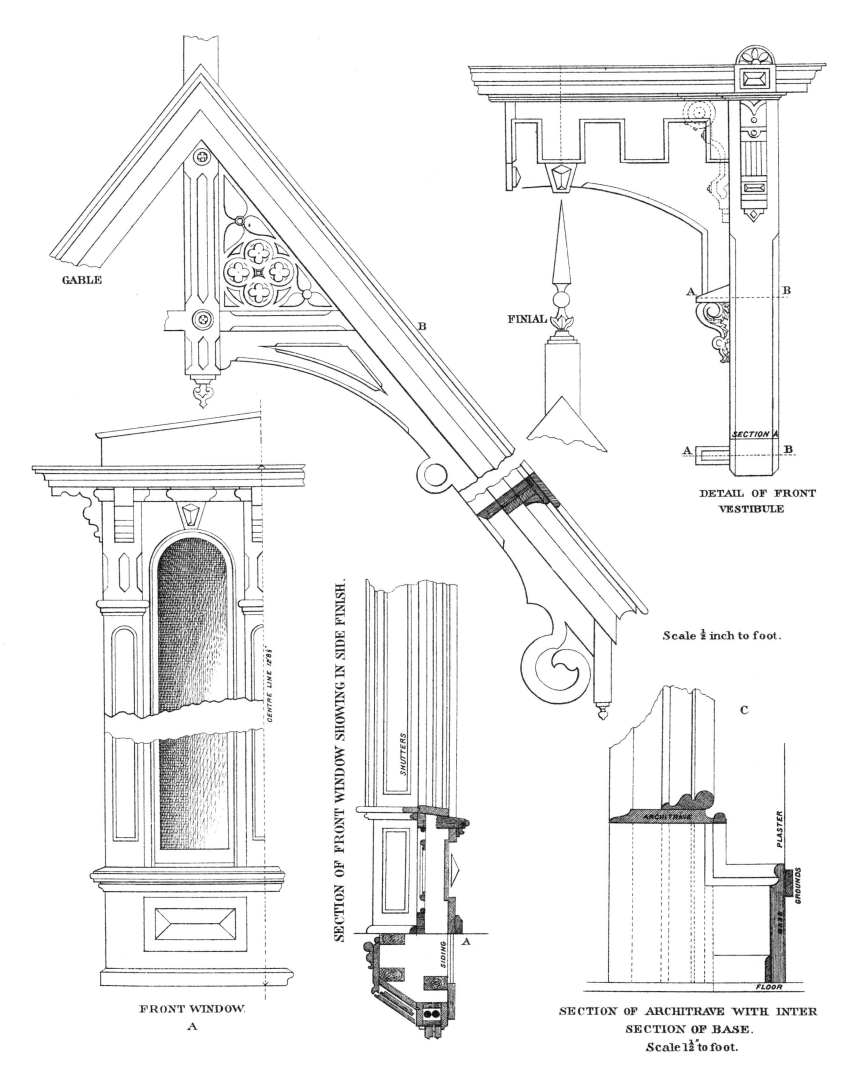

GABLE

FINIAL

DETAIL OF FRONT
VESTIBULE

Scale ½ inch to foot.

CENTRE LINE 128⅝"

FRONT WINDOW.

A

SECTION OF FRONT WINDOW SHOWING IN SIDE FINISH.

SHUTTERS

SIDING

A

SECTION A

A

B

A

B

C

ARCHITRAVE

PLASTER

GROUNDS

FLOOR

SECTION OF ARCHITRAVE WITH INTER
SECTION OF BASE.
Scale 1½" to foot.

PLATE 12

PLATES 13, 14.

DESIGN FOR A CHEAP RESIDENCE WITH FRENCH ROOF.

G. B. CROFF, Architect, Fort Edward, N. Y.

Plate 13. Contains the front elevation, first floor plan, and details of Cornice, Balustrade, Canopy, Window-caps, &c.

Plate 14. Shows the side elevation, plan of second floor and details for front and rear Verandah.

Scale of elevations and plans one-eighth of one inch to the foot. Details three-fourth of one inch to the foot.

This dwelling has recently been erected for John D. Bancroft, Cashier of the First National Bank of Ballston Spa, N. Y. Total cost including Architect's fees $4,000. The design presents a unique and inviting appearance and would voluntarily suggest an outlay of double the amount. The roof is covered with slate of the best quality. The frame is balloon constructed from two by four wallstrips and covered with good quality pine clap-boards, laying four inches to the weather. The first story is filled in with soft brick well laid in lime mortar. The floors are best quality Canada spruce. The exterior and interior details are of pine. The windows are hung with weights and supplied with finely finished inside blinds. The basement contains a hot-air furnace with four, nine by fourteen registers.

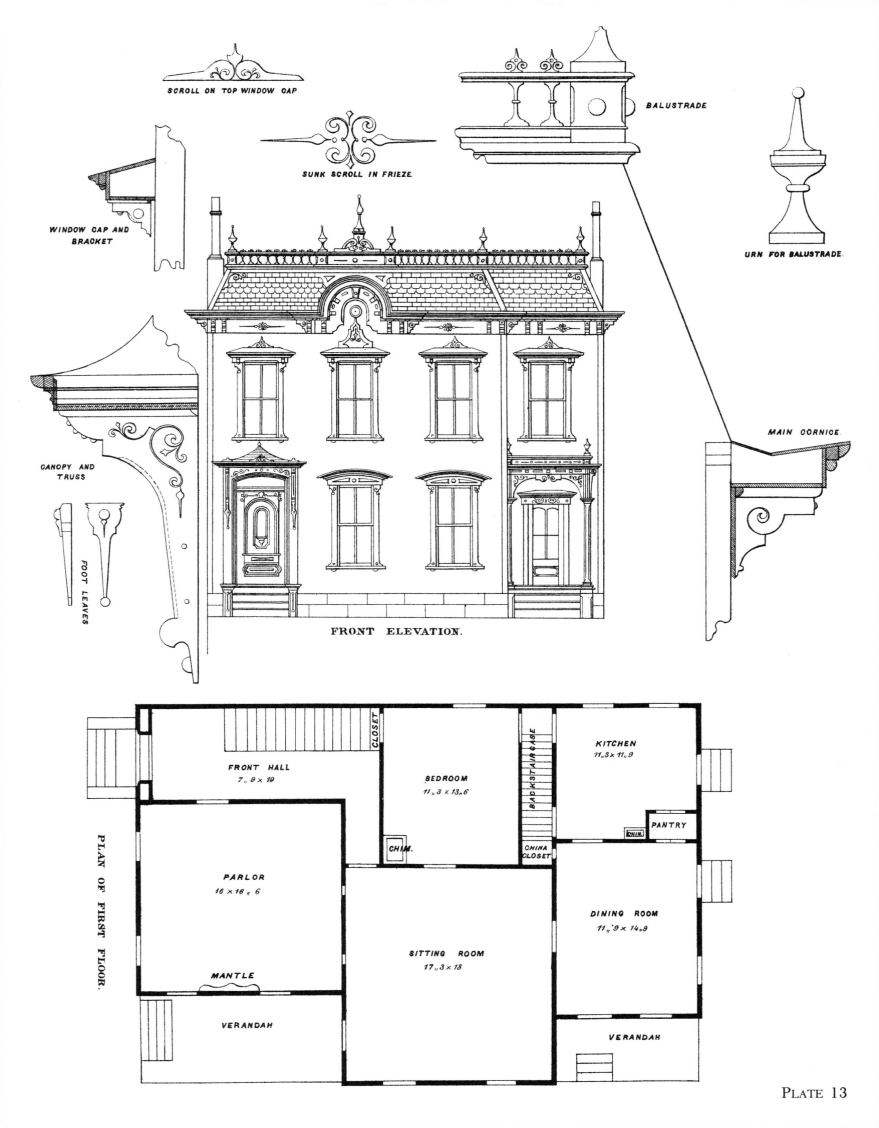

SCROLL ON TOP WINDOW CAP.

BALUSTRADE

SUNK SCROLL IN FRIEZE.

WINDOW CAP AND BRACKET

URN FOR BALUSTRADE.

CANOPY AND TRUSS

FOOT LEAVES

MAIN CORNICE.

FRONT ELEVATION.

PLAN OF FIRST FLOOR.

CLOSET

FRONT HALL
7„9 × 19

BEDROOM
11„3 × 13„6

BACKSTAIR CASE

KITCHEN
11„3 × 11„9

CHIM.

CHINA CLOSET

CHIN. PANTRY

PARLOR
16 × 16„6

SITTING ROOM
17„3 × 18

DINING ROOM
11„9 × 14„9

MANTLE

VERANDAH

VERANDAH

PLATE 13

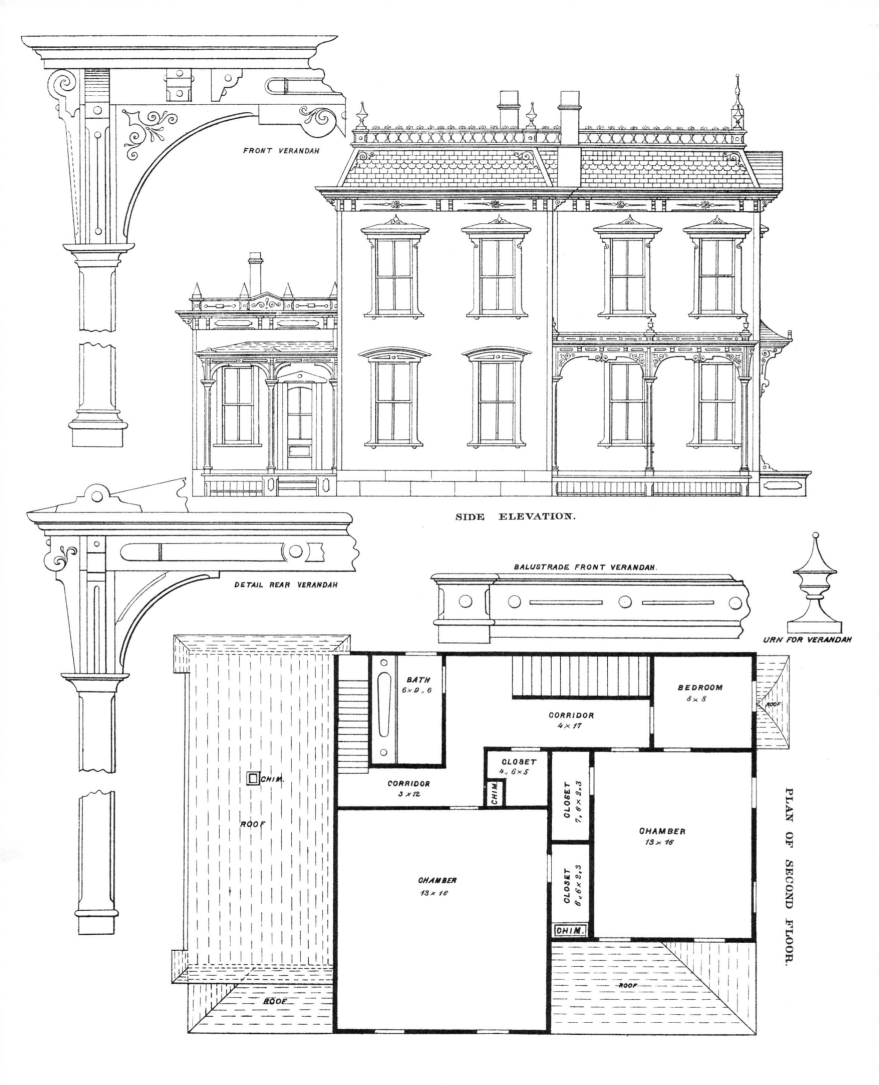

FRONT VERANDAH

SIDE ELEVATION.

DETAIL REAR VERANDAH

BALUSTRADE FRONT VERANDAH.

URN FOR VERANDAH

ROOF

CHIM.

ROOF

CHAMBER
13 × 16

CORRIDOR
3 × 12

BATH
6 × 9 „ 6

CORRIDOR
4 × 17

BEDROOM
8 × 8

ROOF

CLOSET
4 „ 6 × 5

CHIM.

CLOSET
7, 6 × 2, 3

CHAMBER
13 × 16

CLOSET
6 „ 6 × 2, 3

CHIM.

ROOF

PLAN OF SECOND FLOOR.

PLATE 14

PLATE 15.

DESIGN FOR A TWO STORY BRICK SUBURBAN RESIDENCE.

E. E. MYERS, Architect, Springfield, Ill.

Fig. 1. Front elevation.

Fig. 2. Side elevation.

Fig. 3. First floor plan, containing Hall, Parlor, Dining and Sitting-room, Kitchen and Pantry.

Fig. 4. Second floor, containing Guests' and Family rooms, Bath-room, two Bed-rooms and Servants' room.

Fig. 5. Basement plan. Scale sixteen feet to one inch. Cost $4,500.

FRONT ELEVATION

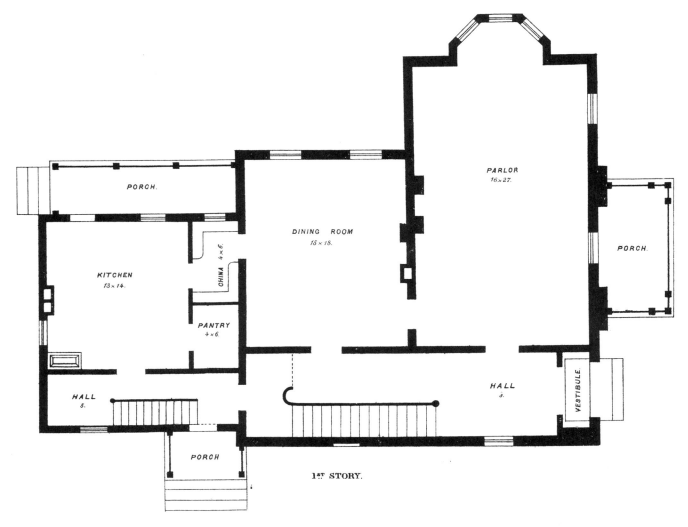

PORCH.

KITCHEN
13 × 14.

CHINA 4 × 6.

PANTRY
4 × 6.

DINING ROOM
15 × 18.

PARLOR
16 × 27.

PORCH.

HALL
5.

HALL
5.

VESTIBULE.

PORCH

1ST STORY.

PLATE 16   [plate reduced 10 per cent in this reprint edition]

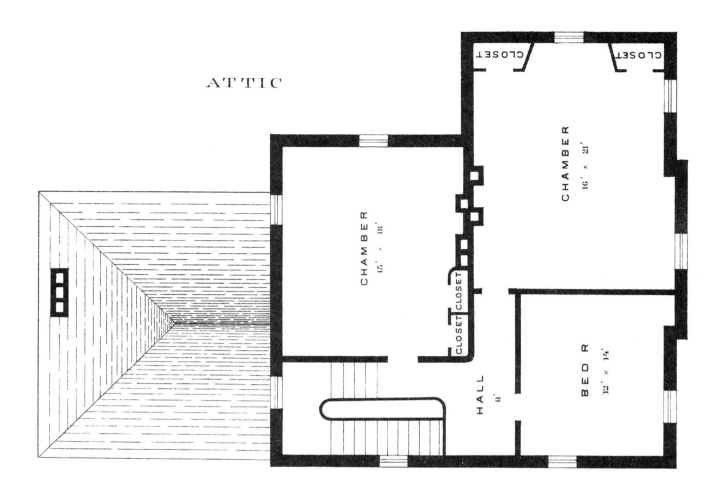

ATTIC

CHAMBER
15' × 18'

CHAMBER
16' × 21'

CLOSET

CLOSET

CLOSET

CLOSET

HALL
8'

BED R.
12' × 14'

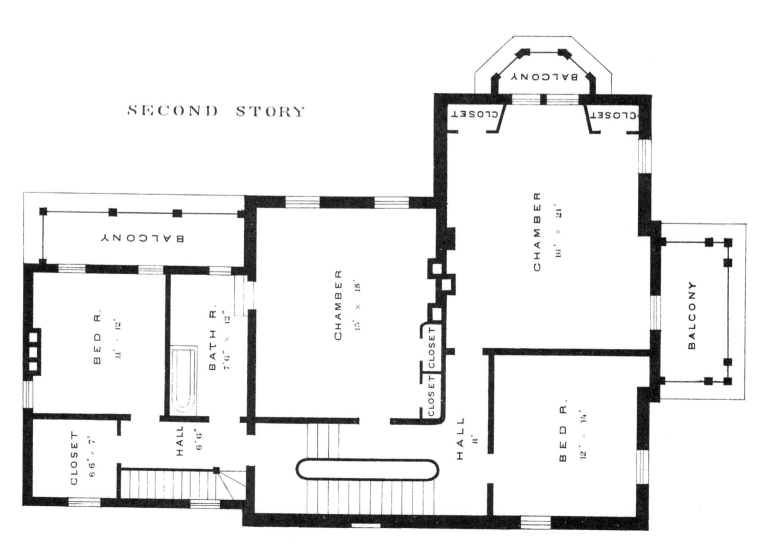

SECOND STORY

BALCONY

BED R.
11' × 12'

BATH R.
7'6" × 12'

CLOSET
6'6" × 7'

HALL
6'6"

CHAMBER
15' × 18'

CLOSET

CLOSET

CHAMBER
16' × 21'

BALCONY

CLOSET

CLOSET

BALCONY

HALL
8'

BED R.
12' × 14'

PLATE 17

PLATES 18, 19.

DESIGN OF SUBURBAN RESIDENCE.

E. E. MYERS, Architect, Springfield, Ill.

Plate 18.   Front elevation and first floor plan.

Plate 19.   Side elevation and second floor plan.   Scale one-eighth of one inch to the foot.

This dwelling has been recently erected for W. B. Corneau, of Springfield, Ill.   Cost $10,000.

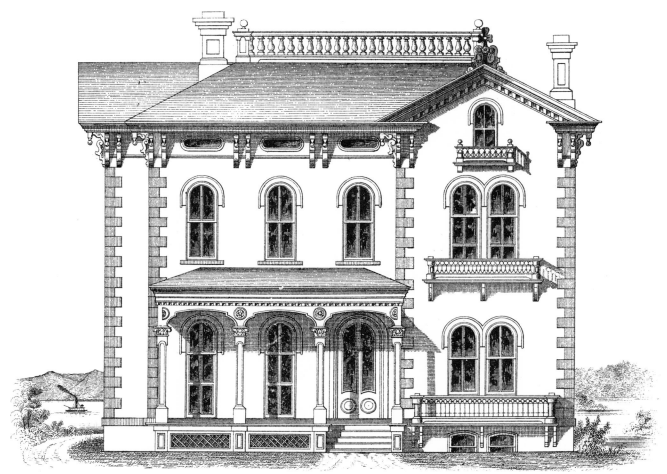

FRONT ELEVATION.

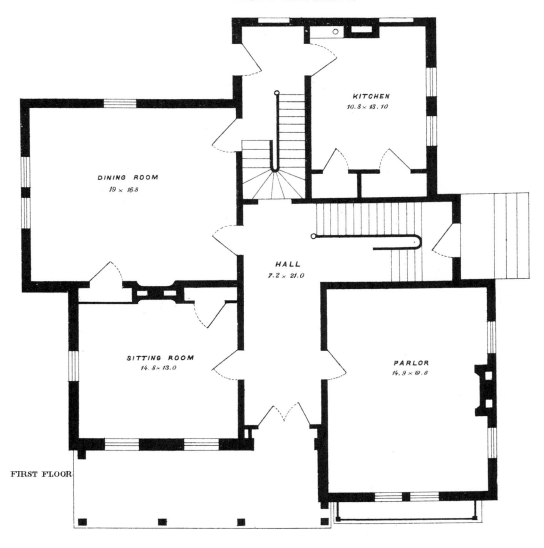

KITCHEN
10.8 × 13.10

DINING ROOM
19 × 16.8

HALL
7.2 × 21.0

SITTING ROOM
14.8 × 13.0

PARLOR
14.9 × 19.6

FIRST FLOOR

[plate reduced 10 per cent in this reprint edition] PLATE 18

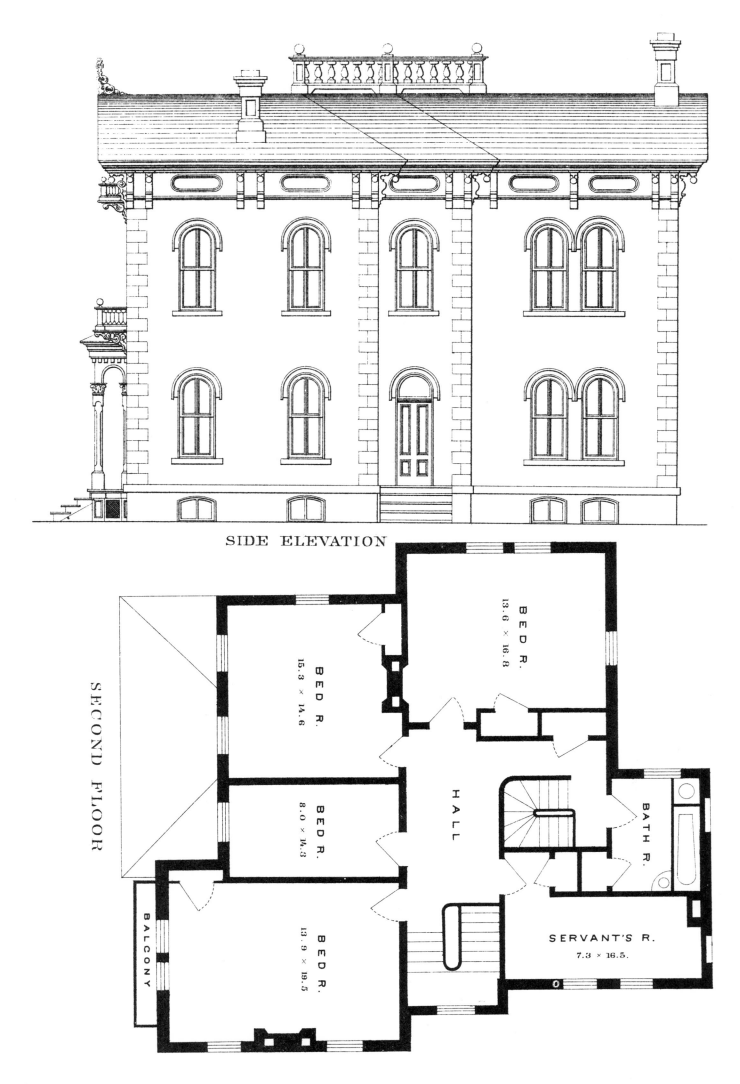

SIDE ELEVATION

SECOND FLOOR

BED R.
13.6 × 16.8

BED R.
15.3 × 14.6

BED R.
8.0 × 14.3

HALL

BATH R.

BED R.
13.9 × 19.5

BALCONY

SERVANT'S R.
7.3 × 16.5.

PLATE 19

PLATES 20, 21, 22.

DESIGN FOR A FIRST CLASS DWELLING.

E. BOYDON & SON, Architects, Worcester, Mass.

Plate 20. Front elevation.

Plate 21. Rear elevation and ground plan.

Plate 22. Side elevation and chamber plan.

This house has been built for Mr. J. A. Hovey, Ballston Spa, N. Y., and is one of the best residences in that section of the country.   The cost was $30,000.

Scale of plans and elevations one inch to twelve feet.

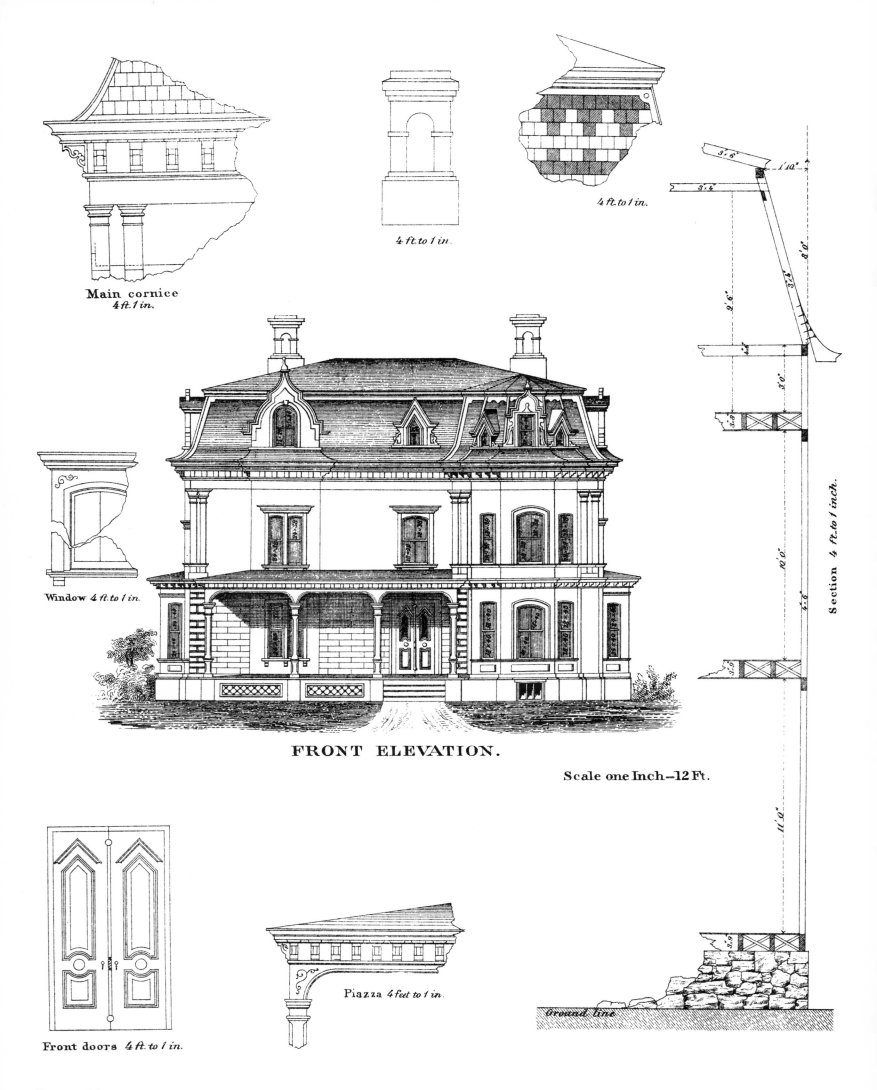

Main cornice
4 ft. 1 in.

4 ft. to 1 in.

4 ft. to 1 in.

Window 4 ft. to 1 in.

Section 4 ft. to 1 inch.

FRONT ELEVATION.

Scale one Inch—12 Ft.

Front doors 4 ft. to 1 in.

Piazza 4 feet to 1 in.

Ground line

PLATE 20

REAR ELEVATION

AND

GROUND PLAN

Scale 1-inch-12 ft.

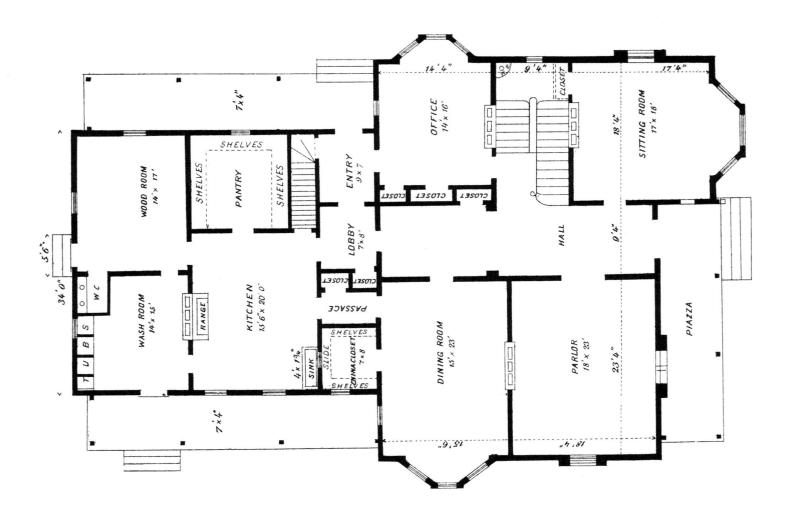

PLATE 21

SIDE ELEVATION.

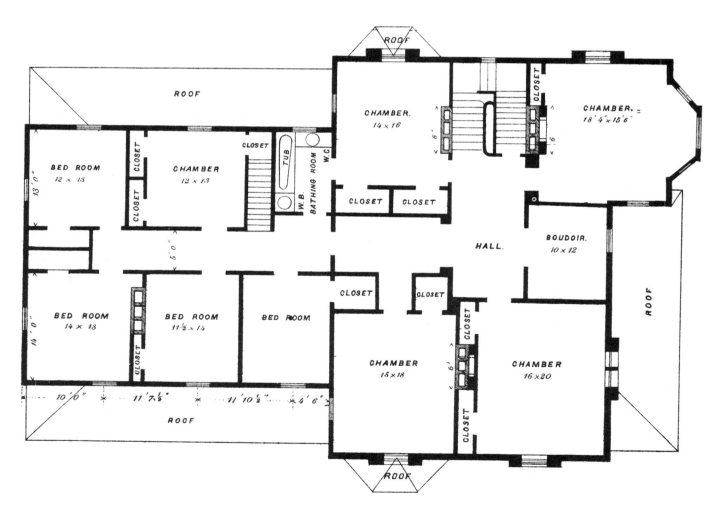

CHAMBER PLAN.

Scale 1 inch = 12 feet.

PLATE 22

PLATES 23, 24, 25, 26.

DESIGN FOR A FARM HOUSE.

E. E. MYERS, Architect, Springfield, Ill.

Plate 23. Shows the front view.

Plate 24. First floor plan.

Plate 25. Side view.

Plate 26. Second floor plan.

This residence has been erected for Lewis Thomas, of Montgomery County, Ill., on a farm, containing 2,000 acres. Cost $30,000.

Scale of elevations and plans three thirty-second of one inch to the foot.

FRONT VIEW

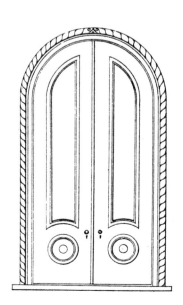

Scale of Details: ¼ of 1 inch to 1 foot.

PLATE 23

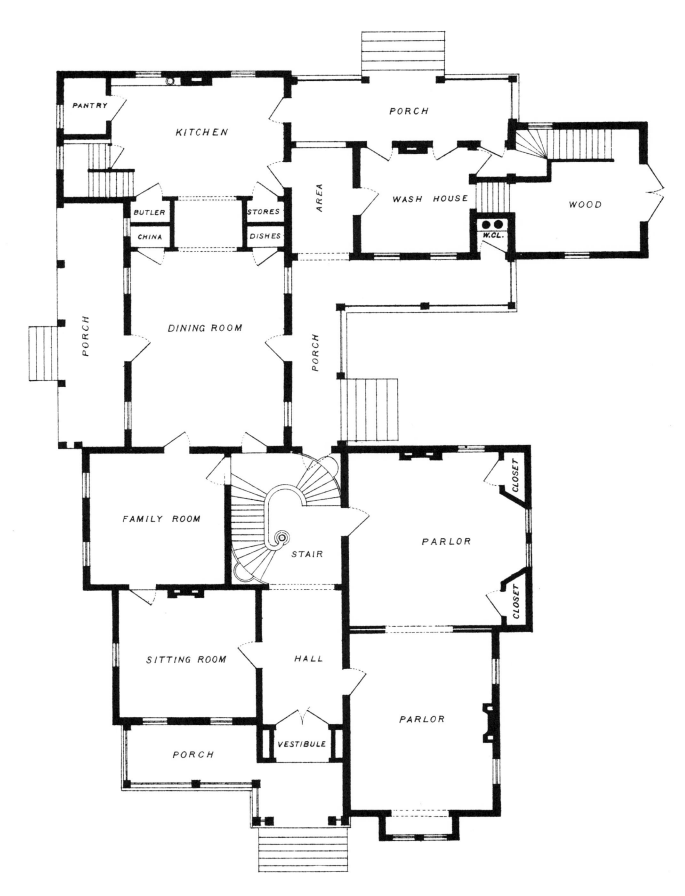

PANTRY

KITCHEN

PORCH

WASH HOUSE

WOOD

AREA

BUTLER

STORES

CHINA

DISHES

W.CL.

PORCH

DINING ROOM

PORCH

FAMILY ROOM

STAIR

PARLOR

CLOSET

CLOSET

SITTING ROOM

HALL

PARLOR

PORCH

VESTIBULE

FIRST FLOOR PLAN.

PLATE 24

SIDE VIEW.

Details ¼ of 1 inch to 1 foot.

PLATE 25

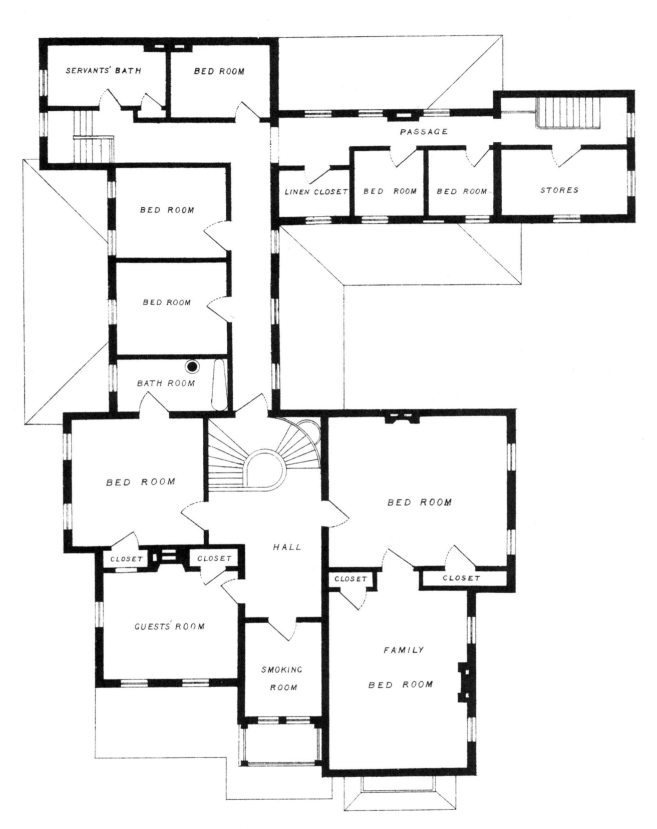

SECOND FLOOR.

PLATE 26

PLATES 27, 28,

DESIGN FOR A HANDSOME SUBURBAN RESIDENCE.

F. Wm. READER, Architect, 307 Locust Street, St. Louis, Mo.

Plate 27. Front elevation.

Plate 28. Plans of Basement, first floor, second floor and attic: a, denotes range; b b, dumb waiters; c c c c, wash troughs; d d, waste soil pipes; e e e e, dining-room closets; f f, flues of range and furnace; g g, hot air flues; h h, hot air registers or grates; i i i i, ventilating ducts; k k k k, chamber closets; k, hall closets; k k, closet under stairs; l l, water-closets in basement; l l l, water-closets on second floor; m m m m m, wash-stands; m, hydrant and sink.

Scale of elevation, one-eighth of one inch to the foot; scale of plan, one-sixteenth of one inch to the foot. Cost $21,000.

FRONT ELEVATION.

Details ¼ of 1 inch to 1 foot.

PLATE 27

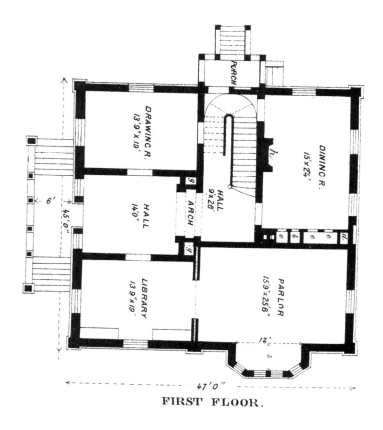

FIRST FLOOR.

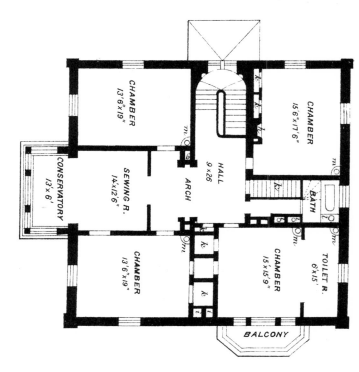

SECOND FLOOR.

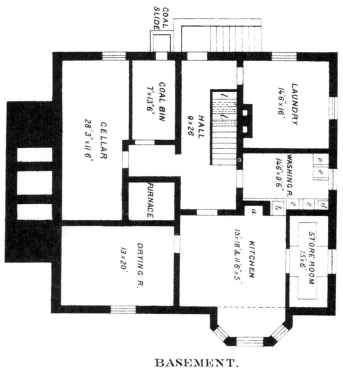

BASEMENT.

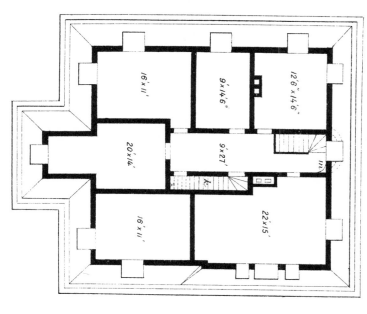

ATTIC.

PLATE 28

PLATE 29.

MODEL DESIGN FOR A CHEAP CITY DWELLING.

C. BOLIN STARK, Architect, Philadelphia, Pa.

This Plate shows the front elevation, section and plans of a city residence of moderate cost. The basement has a kitchen, closet, and coal cellar; the first story ante-room, dining-room and closets; the second story contains library and parlor; third story—bed-room, dressing-room, bath-room and closet.

Scale—one-eighth of one inch to the foot. Cost, built of brick and plainly furnished, $2,000

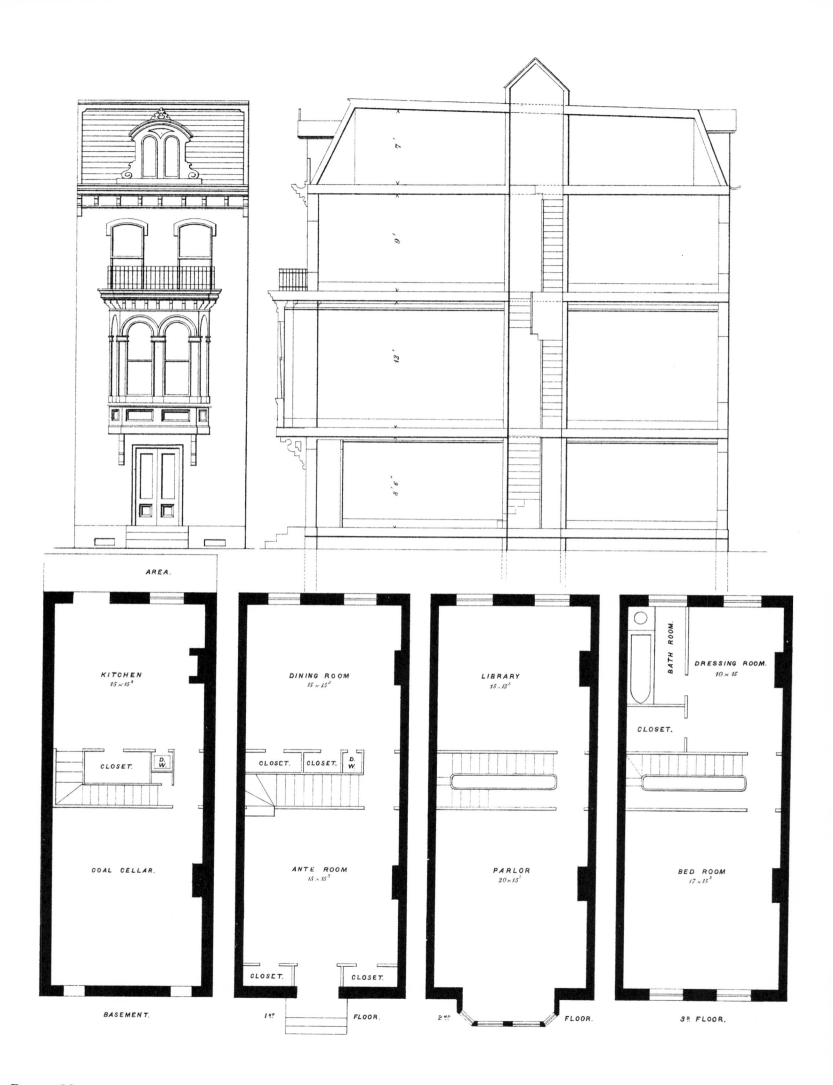

AREA.

KITCHEN
15 × 15³

CLOSET. D. W.

COAL CELLAR.

BASEMENT.

DINING ROOM
15 × 15³

CLOSET. CLOSET. D. W.

ANTE ROOM
15 × 15³

CLOSET. CLOSET.

1ST FLOOR.

LIBRARY
15 × 15³

PARLOR
20 × 15³

2ND FLOOR.

BATH ROOM.

DRESSING ROOM.
10 × 15

CLOSET.

BED ROOM
17 × 15³

3D FLOOR.

PLATE 29   [plate reduced 10 per cent in this reprint edition]

PLATES 30, 31.

PERSPECTIVE VIEW, FRONT ELEVATION AND PLAN FOR A FIRST-CLASS STABLE.

E. BOYDEN & SON, Architects, Worcester, Mass.

This stable has been recently erected for a gentleman at Worcester, Mass. The style of his residence is Elizabethan, and the stable is made to correspond. Cost $5,000.

PLATE 30

STABLE

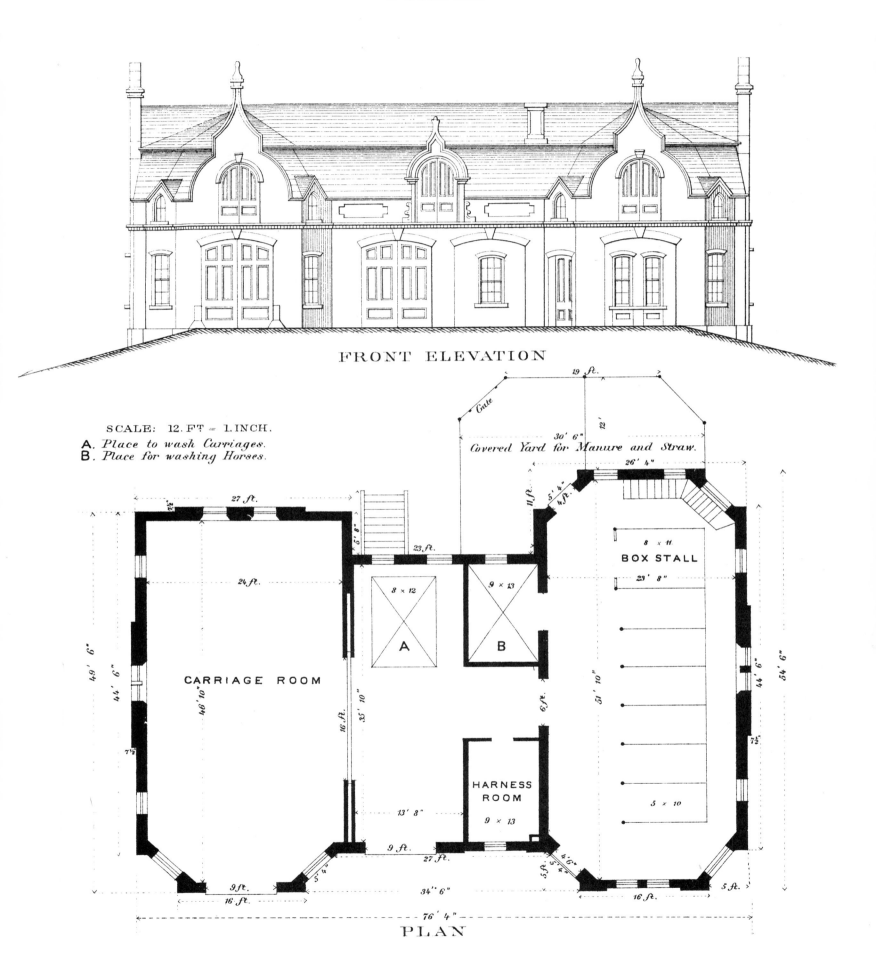

FRONT ELEVATION

SCALE: 12. FT = 1. INCH.
A. *Place to wash Carriages.*
B. *Place for washing Horses.*

19 ft.

Gate

30' 6"   12'

Covered Yard for Manure and Straw.

26' 4"

BOX STALL

8 × 11

23' 8"

27 ft.

24 ft.

8 × 12   9 × 13

A   B

5 × 10

CARRIAGE ROOM

46' 10"

23 ft.

35' 10"

16 ft.

6 ft.

51' 10"

44' 6"   54' 6"

49' 6"

44' 6"

7½

7½

HARNESS ROOM

9 × 13

13' 8"

9 ft.   27 ft.

9 ft.

16 ft.

34'' 6"

5 ft.

16 ft.   5 ft.

76' 4"

PLAN

PLATE 31

PLATE 32.

ELEVATIONS AND PLANS FOR A CARRIAGE-HOUSE AND STABLE.

E. E. MYERS, Architect, Springfield, Ill.

Fig. 1. Front elevation.

Fig. 2. Side elevation.

Fig. 3. Plan of first floor.

Scale, eight feet to one inch. Cost, built of brick and covered with slate, $2,700.

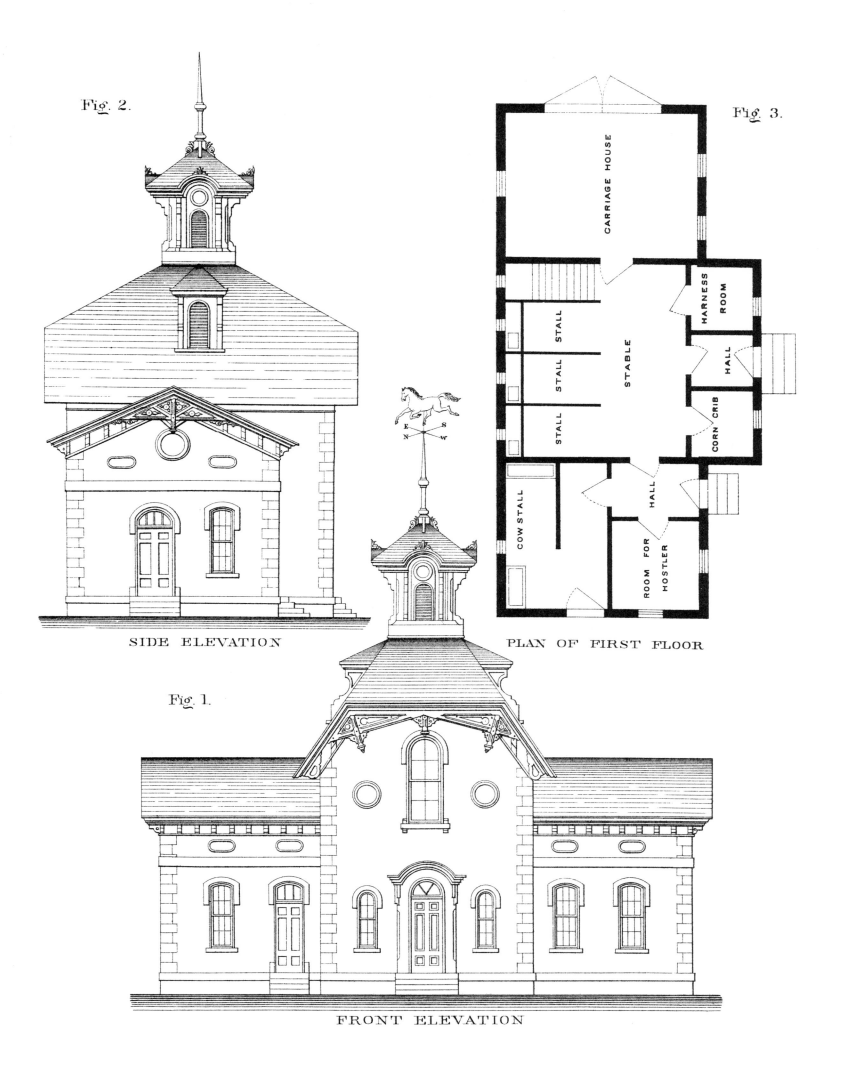

Fig. 2.

SIDE ELEVATION

Fig. 3.

CARRIAGE HOUSE

HARNESS ROOM

STALL

STALL

STALL

STALL

STABLE

HALL

CORN CRIB

COW STALL

ROOM FOR HOSTLER

HALL

E S

N W

PLAN OF FIRST FLOOR

Fig. 1.

FRONT ELEVATION

PLATE 33.

ELEVATION OF BLOCK OF TWO STORE-FRONTS.

E. E. MYERS, Architect, Springfield, Ill.

This block has been designed for the Hon. J. C. Conklin, of Springfield, Ill

Scale, one-eighth of one inch to the foot.   Cost $16,000.

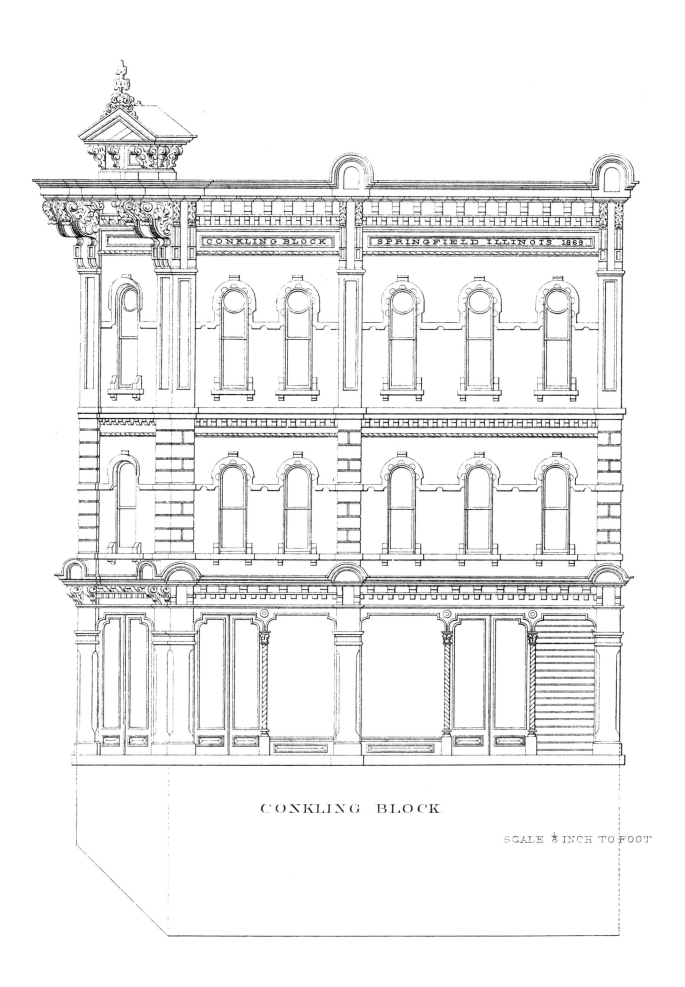

CONKLING BLOCK

SCALE ⅛ INCH TO FOOT

PLATE 33

PLATE 34.

DESIGNS FOR STREET FRONTS FOR STORES.

G. B. CROFF, Architect, Fort Edward, N. Y.

Design A, shows a store front prepared for Thomas Eldridge, to be built at Fort Edward.

Design B, has been executed in the village of Ballston Spa, N.Y., for John J. Luther, Esq.

A and B are drawn on the scale of three-sixteenth of one inch to the foot.

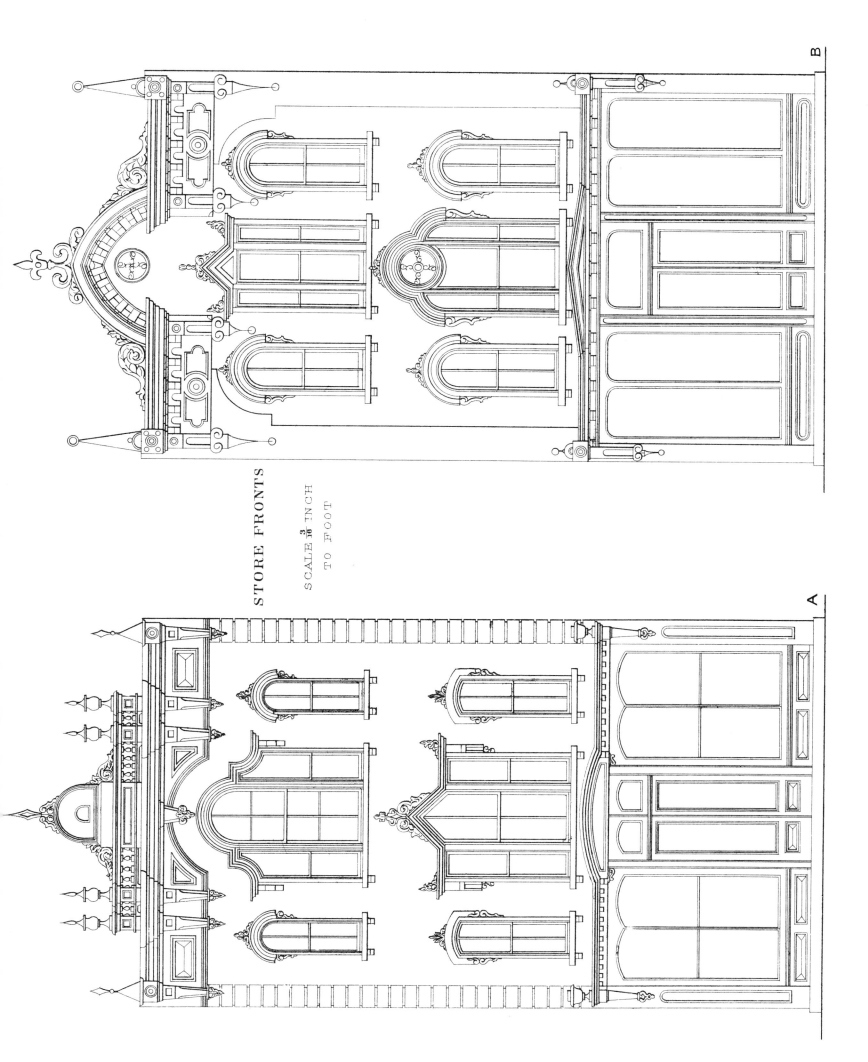

STORE FRONTS

SCALE $\frac{3}{16}$ INCH TO FOOT

B

A

PLATE 34

PLATE 35.

DESIGNS FOR FOUR STORES.

E. E. MYERS, Architect, Springfield, Ill.

This block of stores is erected at Jacksonville, Ill.
Scale of elevation, one-eighth of one inch to the foot.   Cost $30,000.

THE FRONT ELEVATION OF AYERS BLOCK AT JACKSONVILLE ILL.

AYERS' BLOCK
JACKSONVILLE.

1868.

1868.

PLATE 35

PLATE 36.

DESIGN FOR A FRAME SCHOOL-HOUSE.

E. E. MYERS, Architect, Springfield, Ill.

This Plate shows the front elevation and plans for a two-story frame school-house, now being erected at Loami, Ill.

Scale of elevation, one-eighth of one inch to the foot; scale of plans, one-sixteenth of one inch to the foot.   Cost $6,000.

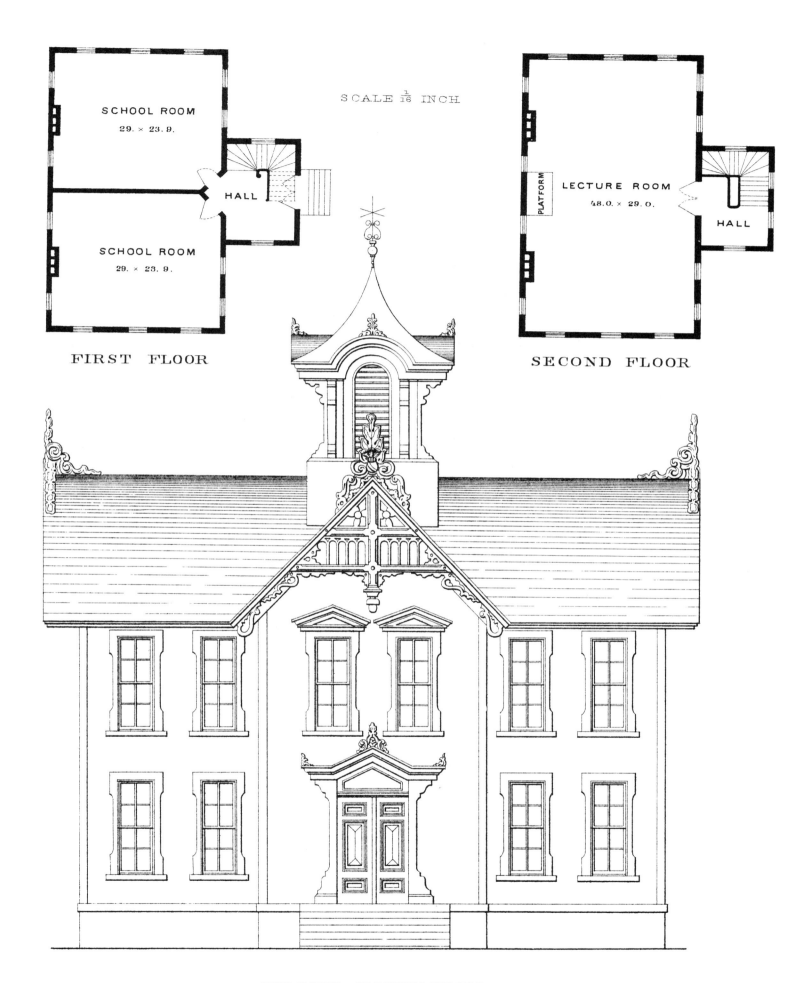

SCALE $\frac{1}{16}$ INCH

SCHOOL ROOM
29. × 23. 9.

HALL

SCHOOL ROOM
29. × 23. 9.

FIRST FLOOR

PLATFORM

LECTURE ROOM
48. 0. × 29. 0.

HALL

SECOND FLOOR

FRONT ELEVATION

SCALE $\frac{8}{}$ INCH TO FOOT.

PLATE 36

PLATES 37, 38.

DESIGN FOR A BRICK SCHOOL-HOUSE WITH MANSARD ROOF.

THEO. F. LADUE, Architect, Lincoln, Ill.

Plate 37. Shows the front elevation and several details of a school-house now being erected at Lincoln, Ill. A, main cornice; B, tower cornice; C, top of steep roof; D, cornice of dormer windows.

Plate 38. First and third floor plan; the second story is arranged same as the first, with the exception of a school inspector's room over front hall. The building has two entrances, by front and rear; hall fifteen feet wide, with two stairways five feet wide, which communicate with all the rooms. There are four school-rooms on first, and second stories, with large wardrobes and teachers' closet for each room. The wardrobes are so arranged, that there need be no confusion coming in or going out. The third story contains a chapel and two recitation rooms. All the rooms are to be wainscoted with alternate ash and black walnut; and all windows are to be supplied with inside blinds. The walls are red brick trimmed with Milwaukee pressed brick.

The building will be heated and ventilated by Ruttan's system.

The basement is divided into fuel cellars, water-closets, etc.

Scale of plans and elevations, 1-12th of inch to the foot; scale of details, three-fourths of one inch to the foot. Complete cost $37,000.

FRONT ELEVATION.

PLATE 37

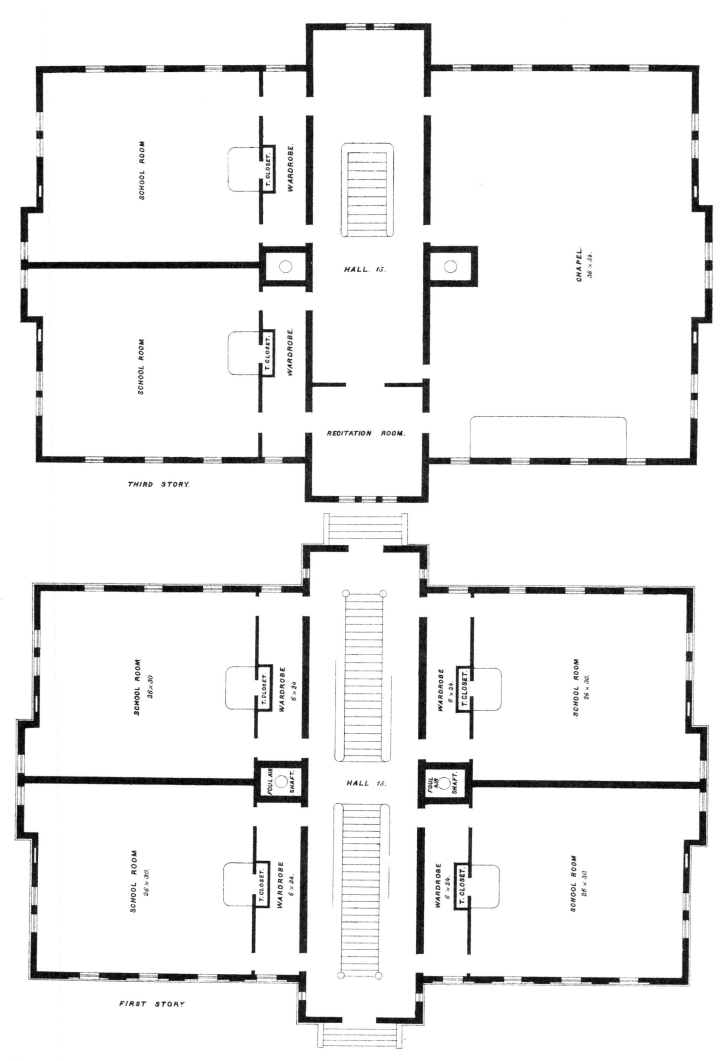

SCHOOL ROOM

SCHOOL ROOM

T. CLOSET.

WARDROBE.

T. CLOSET.

WARDROBE.

HALL. 15.

CHAPEL.
36 × 54.

RECITATION ROOM.

THIRD STORY.

SCHOOL ROOM
26×30

SCHOOL ROOM
26 × 30.

WARDROBE
6 × 24

T. CLOSET.

WARDROBE
6 × 24.

T. CLOSET.

FOUL AIR SHAFT.

FOUL AIR SHAFT.

HALL. 15.

SCHOOL ROOM
26 × 30.

SCHOOL ROOM
26 × 30

T. CLOSET.

WARDROBE
6 × 24.

WARDROBE
6 × 24.

T. CLOSET.

FIRST STORY.

PLATE 38   [plate reduced 10 per cent in this reprint edition]

PLATES 39, 40, 41.

DESIGN FOR A SMALL CHURCH.

Cochrane & Piquenard, Architects, 22, 23 & 24 Lombard Block, Chicago, Ill.

This design is now being erected in the flourishing city of Cheyenne, on the Union Pacific Rail Road. The style of architecture is what is known as modern Gothic. The building is thirty-two by forty-six feet, with a vestibule in front five and one-half by twenty-one feet, and corner tower ten feet square. The same will seat two hundred and ninety-six adults. The height of the interior is thirty-three feet to apex of ceiling, and that of spire eighty feet. The design is for a wooden structure upon a stone foundation.

Scale, eight feet to one inch. The cost will be $8,000.

FRONT ELEVATION.

PLATE 39

SIDE ELEVATION.

PLATE 40

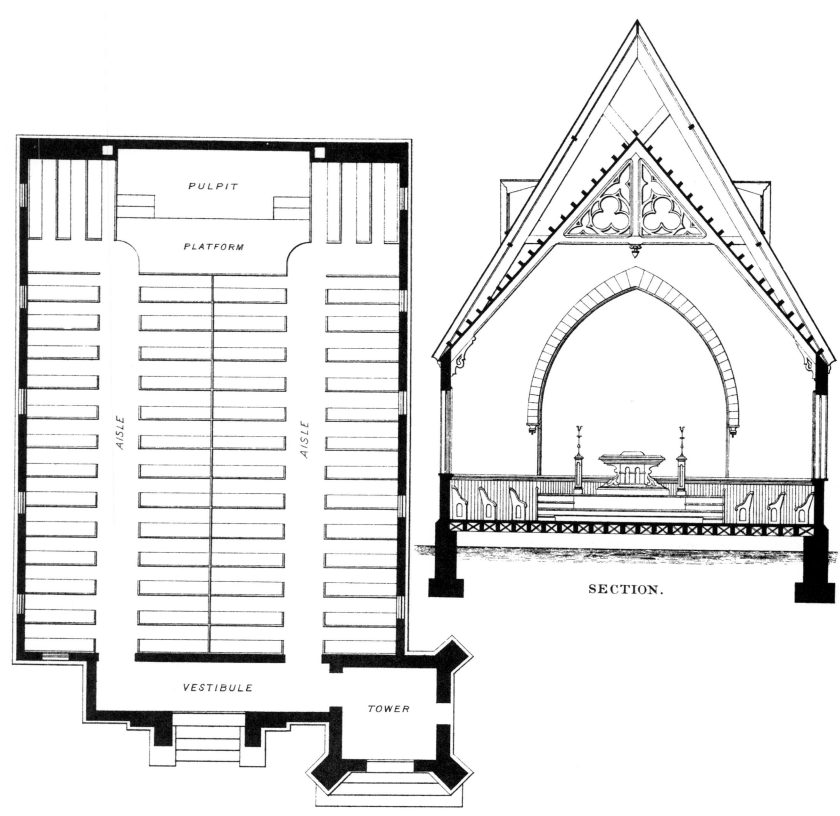

PULPIT

PLATFORM

AISLE

AISLE

VESTIBULE

TOWER

GROUND PLAN.

SECTION.

PLATE 41

PLATE 42.

DESIGN FOR A CHAPEL CHURCH.

LYMAN UNDERWOOD, Architect, 13 Exchange Street, Boston, Mass.

This Plate shows the front elevation and plan of a church edifice, with accommodations for about seven hundred persons. It is intended to be built of stone or brick, with cut stone dressings, although the same design might be carried out in wood. The entrances are numerous and conveniently arranged, as well as amply large. In the front is a vestibule nine feet wide, extending entirely across the building, containing four entrances to the audience room, as well as the stairs to the small gallery above. The audience room is sixty by seventy feet, with a chancel twenty feet wide at the end opposite the principal entrance, containing the pulpit or any other arrangements which denominational peculiarities might require. There are one hundred and thirty-six pews on the principal floor, with five sittings in each. The organ is on one side of the chancel and on the opposite is a minister's retiring room. Access to the audience room is also had through vestibules upon either side, and these vestibules also communicate with the vestry and committee rooms. The vestry is forty by forty-eight feet, the committee rooms each eighteen by twenty feet, communicating with each other by folding or sliding doors, and also with the vestry by the means of sliding sashes in addition to the ordinary doors. Above the committee rooms, and reached by an ample flight of stairs from the vestibule below is an additional room for the use of the ladies of the society. All of these various rooms would be abundantly lighted, and well ventilated. The expense of the building would of necessity vary very much with different localities, and with the amount of cut stone used upon the exterior; but under favorable circumstances it might be built of stone for about $18,000.

The elevation is drawn to a scale of sixteen feet to one inch, and the plan forty-eight feet to one inch.

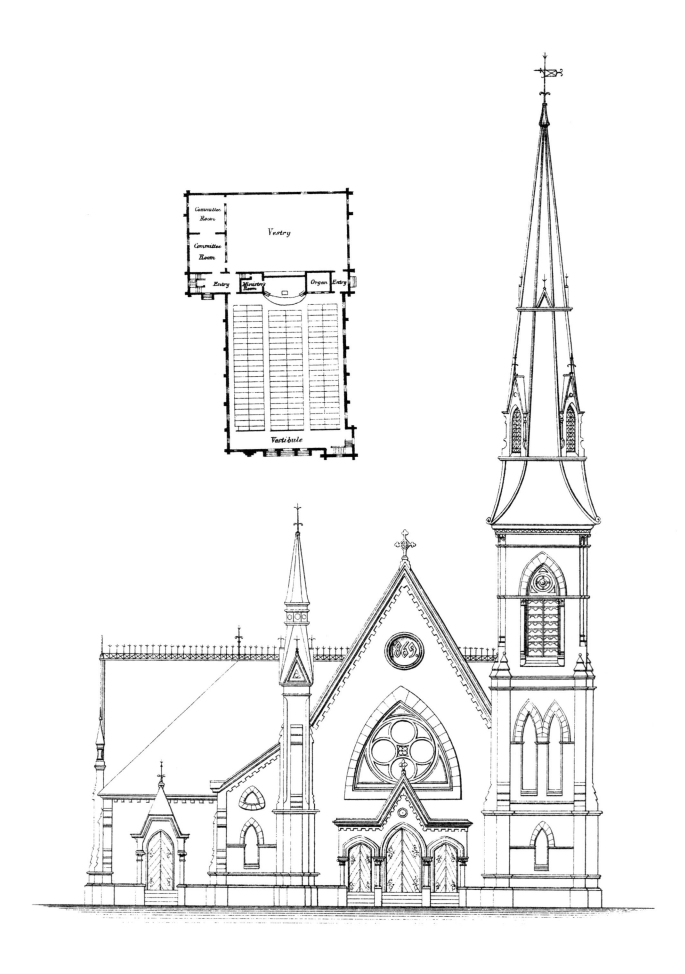

PLATE 42

PLATES 43, 44.

DESIGN FOR A CHURCH.

DAVID S. HOPKINS, Architect, Grand Rapids, Mich.

Plate 43.   Front elevation and basement floor.

Plate 44.   Side elevation and audience floor.

A church after this design is built at Grand Rapids.   It is much admired for its uniqueness and architectural beauty.   It is architecturally Romanesque.   The audience room is forty-six feet wide, sixty feet long, and thirty-five feet high to ceiling, with gallery over front vestibule, extending around from transept to transept.   The audience room will seat six hundred and the gallery two hundred persons.   The front vestibule is thirteen feet wide by forty-six feet long.   Rear vestibule, fourteen feet square.   Rostrum, eleven by thirteen feet.   Choir, nine by eleven feet. Organ recess, ten by eleven feet.   The basement is twelve feet in clear. Lecture-room, about the same size as audience-room, with two class-rooms in front, with sliding doors to the same into lecture-room.   Library and parlor in rear.   Outside dimensions, one hundred and two feet long by sixty-four feet wide, including the projection of the steeple spire, one hundred and fifty-five feet high.   It is built of white brick with brown sandstone trimmings.   Cost $40,000.

FRONT ELEVATION

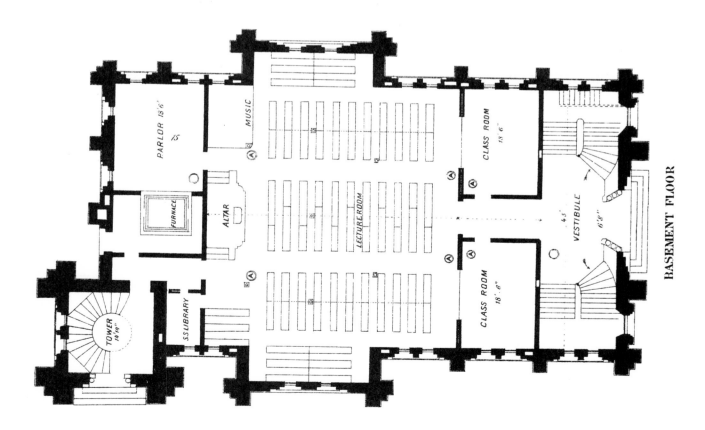

BASEMENT FLOOR

PLATE 43

SIDE ELEVATION.

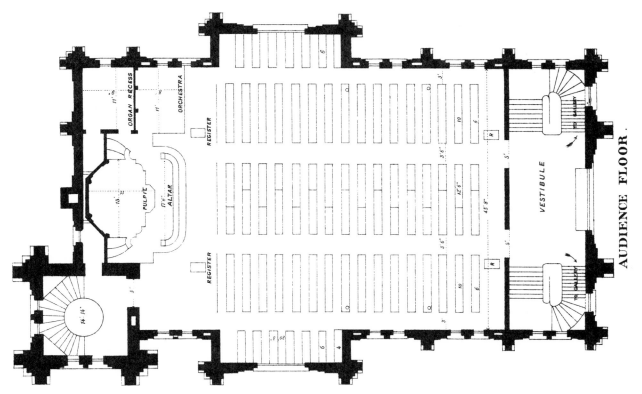

AUDIENCE FLOOR.

PLATE 44

PLATES 45, 46, 47, 48.

DESIGN FOR A FIRST-CLASS COURT-HOUSE.

E. E. MYERS, Architect, Springfield, Ill.

Plate 45. Front elevation.
Plate 46. First floor plan.
Plate 47. Side elevation.
Plate 48. Second floor plan.

This design has been recently executed at Carlinville, Macoupin Co., Ill., and so far as known, it is strictly the only fire-proof building in the country, and is considered the finest county court-house in the United States. The exterior is Athens marble. The windows and door-frames, and the book-cases are all iron. The floors are marble. The interior of the court-room is lined with cast-iron painted in fresco and bronze. The Judge's stand is of granite. The length of building, two hundred and twenty-five feet; width, eighty-six feet; height from ground, eighty-six feet; height of lantern on dome, one hundred and eighty-six feet nine inches. The building throughout is of the finest and best material, no cost having been spared to make it perfect in all its parts.

Scale of elevation and plans, one-eighteenth of one inch to the foot.

FRONT VIEW
OF MACOUPIN COUNTY COURT HOUSE.

Scale ⅛ Inch to Foot.

PLATE 45

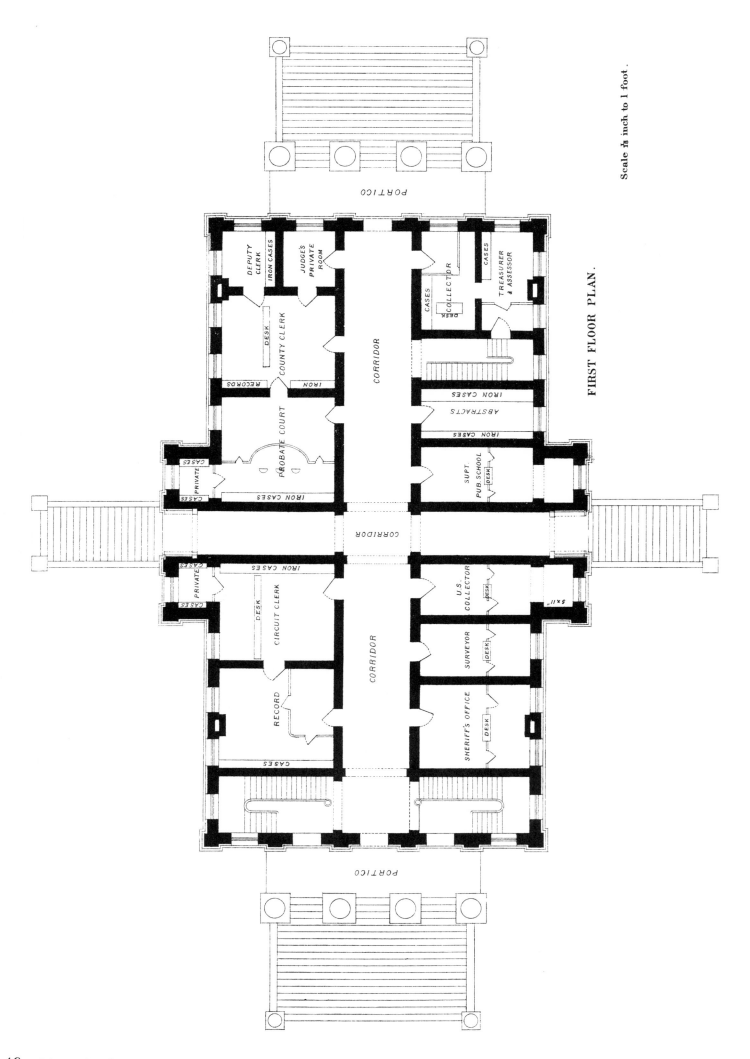

FIRST FLOOR PLAN.

Scale ⅛ inch to 1 foot.

PORTICO

DEPUTY CLERK

IRON CASES

JUDGE'S PRIVATE ROOM

DESK

COUNTY CLERK

RECORDS

IRON

CASES

PRIVATE

CASES

PROBATE COURT

IRON CASES

CORRIDOR

CORRIDOR

CASES

COLLECTOR

DESK

CASES

TREASURER & ASSESSOR

IRON CASES

ABSTRACTS

IRON CASES

SUPT. PUB. SCHOOL

DESK

CASES

PRIVATE

IRON CASES

CIRCUIT CLERK

DESK

RECORD

CASES

CORRIDOR

U.S. COLLECTOR

DESK

SURVEYOR

DESK

SHERIFF'S OFFICE

DESK

5 x 11"

PORTICO

PLATE 46   [plate reduced 10 per cent in this reprint edition]

SIDE VIEW OF MACOUPIN COUNTY COURT HOUSE.

Scale 1/18 inch to 1 foot.

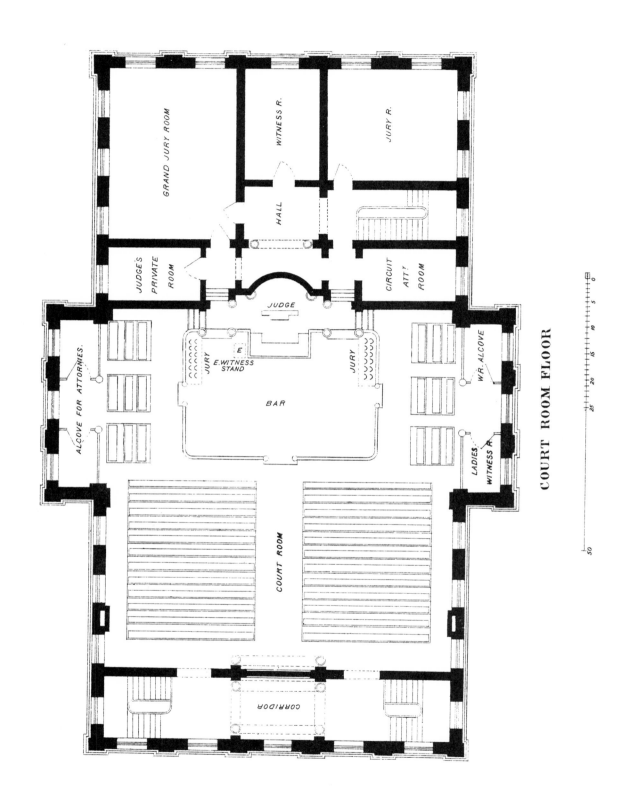

GRAND JURY ROOM

WITNESS R.

JURY R.

HALL

JUDGE'S PRIVATE ROOM

CIRCUIT ATT.Y ROOM

JUDGE

ALCOVE FOR ATTORNIES.

JURY

E
E.WITNESS STAND

JURY

W.R. ALCOVE

BAR

LADIES WITNESS R.

COURT ROOM

CORRIDOR

COURT ROOM FLOOR

0 5 10 15 20 25 50

PLATE 48

PLATES 49, 50, 51.

DESIGN OF BAY COUNTY COURT-HOUSE, BAY CITY, MICH.

Cyrus K. Porter, Architect, Buffalo, N.Y.

Plate 49. Fig. 1, Front elevation.

Fig. 2. Plan of first floor. A, Hall with stairways at each end of main hall, leading to court-rooms above; B, Supervisors' room; C, County clerk's office, with private office; E, D, County treasurer's office, with private office; G, Sheriff's office; H, Clerk of court's office; B, might be used as office of Probate Judge, as either C or D would answer for Board of Supervisors. The rooms in this story are all fourteen feet high in the clear. Safes, I, I, are provided for the offices.

Plate 50. Fig. 3, Side elevation.

Fig. 4. K, Court-room, forty-eight by seventy-one feet, and twenty-two feet high in clear; L, is the Bar containing seats for the judges, jury, and officers of the court; M, Witnesses' waiting-room, with water-closet; N, Counsel room and library; O and P, Jury rooms, one of which is designed to be used as a judge's dressing or retiring-room; they are both supplied with private entrances, water-closets, etc. These rooms are twelve feet high in clear. L, is a stairway leading to an attic above, and from thence to the top of the dome.

The drawings on Plates 49 and 50 are to a scale of sixteen feet to one inch.

Plate 51. Shows the most important details, drawn to a scale of one-half inch to the foot. A, B and F, Portions of dormer windows; C, Main cornice; D, Dome cornice; E, Base and plinth of dome; G, Cornice at angle of roof; H, Cornice of railing around top of dome; L, Chimney top; M and N, Inside finish, one-fourth full size; O, Stairway; P, Wainscoting of court-room; Q and R, Sections of doors, one-half inch to one foot.

The building has a basement of Kingston stone, the superstructure of yellow brick, with sandstone dressings. It is warmed with steam and lighted with gas. The cost was about $42,000, finished in the most substantial manner. Geo. Watkins, of Bay City, was the builder.

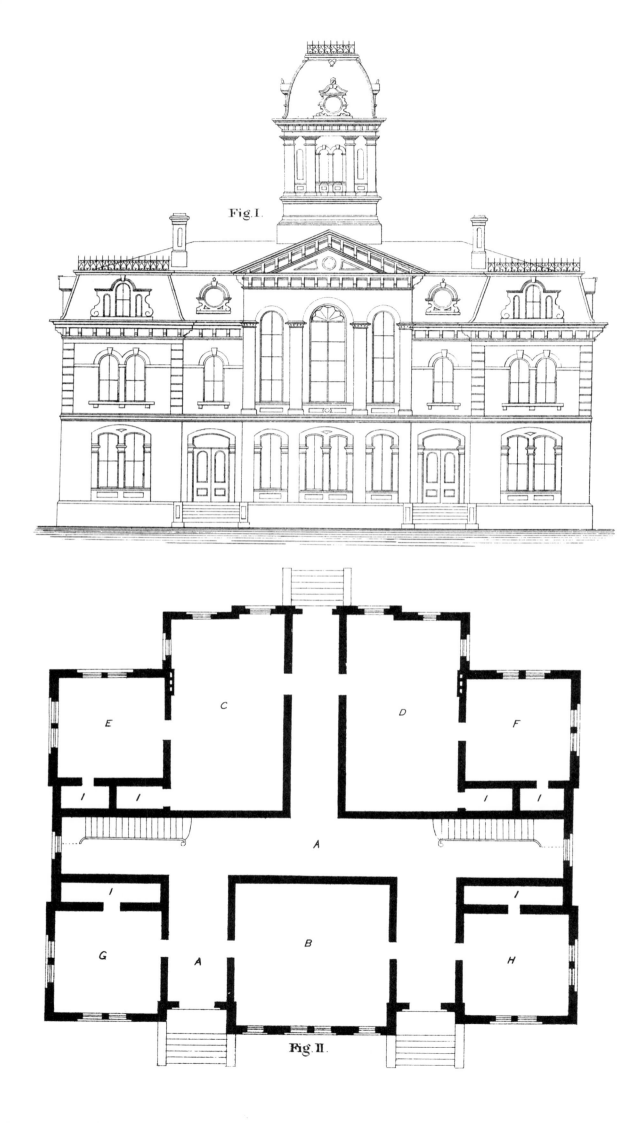

Fig.I.

Fig.II.

PLATE 49

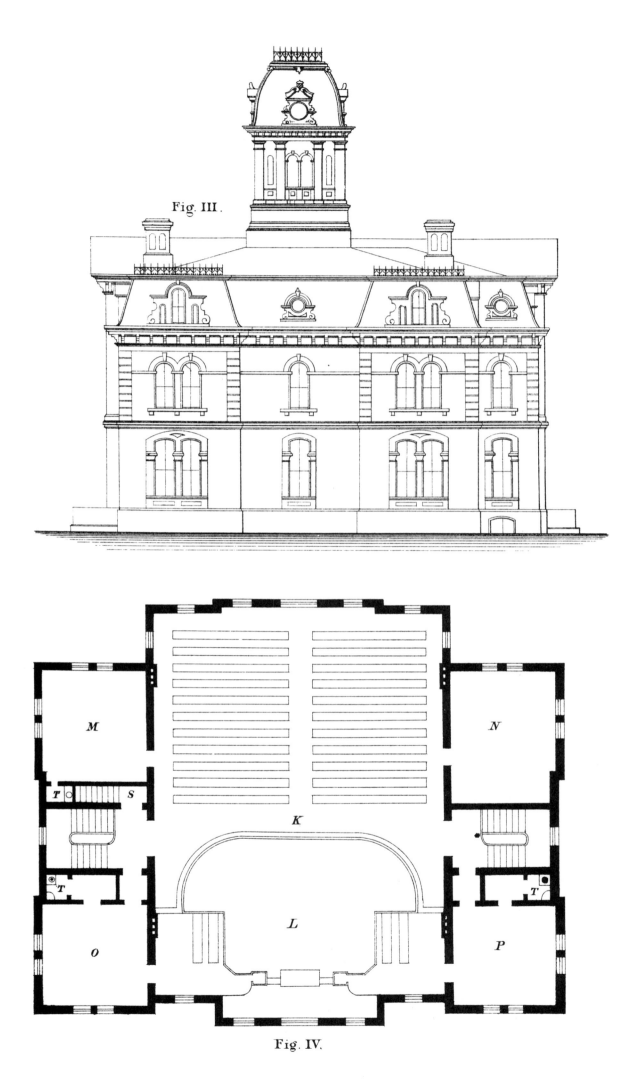

Fig. III.

Fig. IV.

Plate 50

A

C

B

F

D

E

I

K

L

M

¼ full size.

G

H

Q

R

½ inch = 1 foot.

N

O

P

¼ full size.

Scale ½ inch = 1 foot.

PLATE 51 [plate reduced 10 per cent in this reprint edition]

STABLE

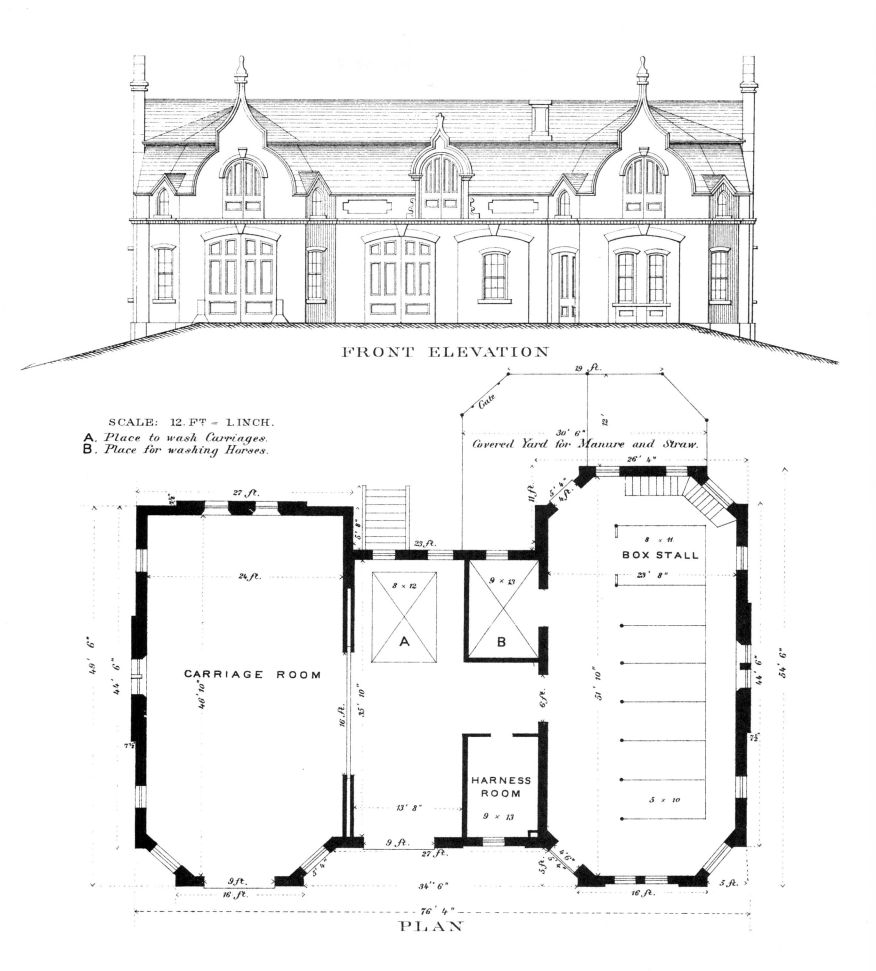

FRONT ELEVATION

SCALE: 12. FT = 1.INCH.
A. *Place to wash Carriages.*
B. *Place for washing Horses.*

Covered Yard for Manure and Straw.

19 ft.

Gate

30' 6"

12'

26' 4"

11 ft.

5' 4"

4 ft.

BOX STALL

8 × 11

27 ft.

6' 8"

23 ft.

29' 8"

49' 6"

44' 6"

54' 6"

24 ft.

8 × 12

9 × 13

A

B

51' 10"

44' 6"

7½

7½

CARRIAGE ROOM

46' 10"

16 ft.

35' 10"

6 ft.

HARNESS ROOM

9 × 13

5 × 10

13' 8"

9 ft.

27 ft.

9 ft.

5' 4"

5 ft.

5' 4"

4' 6"

5 ft.

16 ft.

9 ft.

34' 6"

16 ft.

5 ft.

76' 4"

PLAN

PLATE 31

PLATE 32.

ELEVATIONS AND PLANS FOR A CARRIAGE-HOUSE AND STABLE.

E. E. MYERS, Architect, Springfield, Ill.

Fig. 1. Front elevation.

Fig. 2. Side elevation.

Fig. 3. Plan of first floor.

Scale, eight feet to one inch.   Cost, built of brick and covered with slate, $2,700.

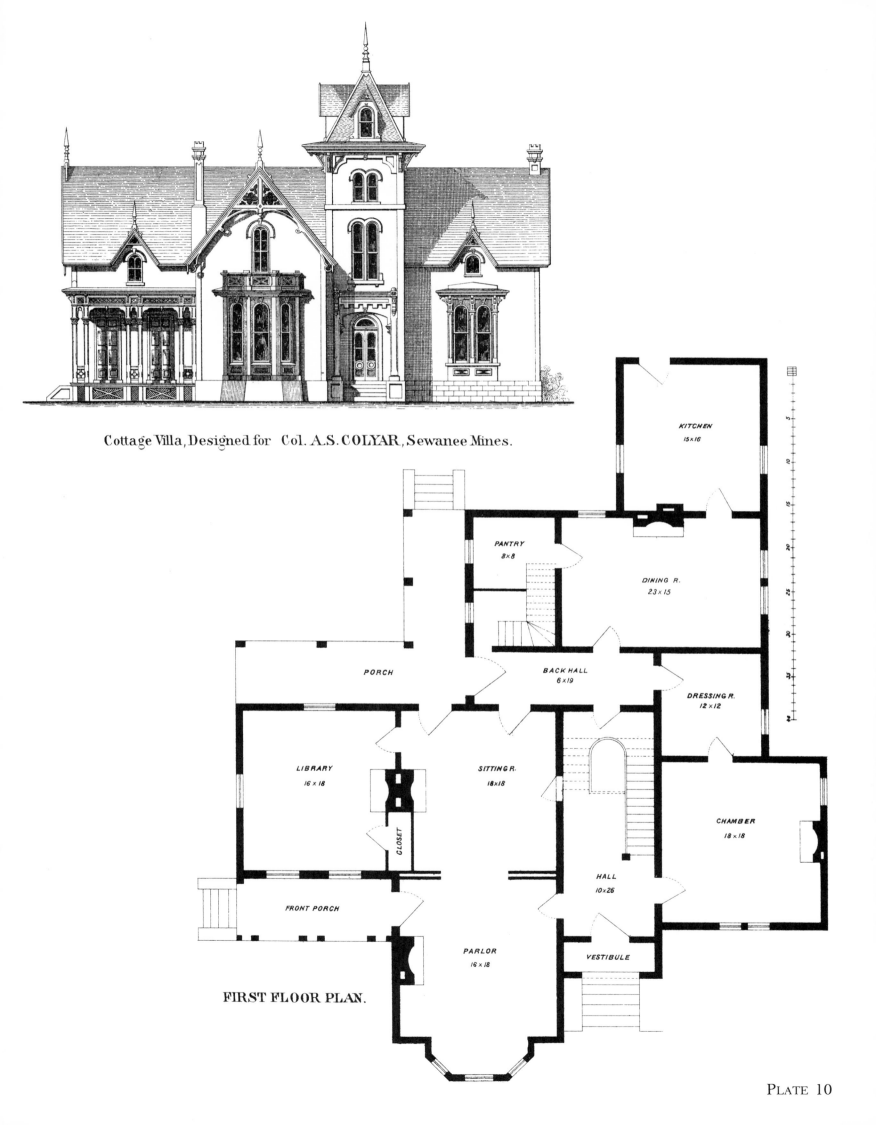

Cottage Villa, Designed for Col. A.S. COLYAR, Sewanee Mines.

FIRST FLOOR PLAN.

KITCHEN
15×16

PANTRY
8×8

DINING R.
23×15

PORCH

BACK HALL
6×19

DRESSING R.
12×12

LIBRARY
16×18

SITTING R.
18×18

CLOSET

CHAMBER
18×18

HALL
10×26

FRONT PORCH

PARLOR
16×18

VESTIBULE

PLATE 10

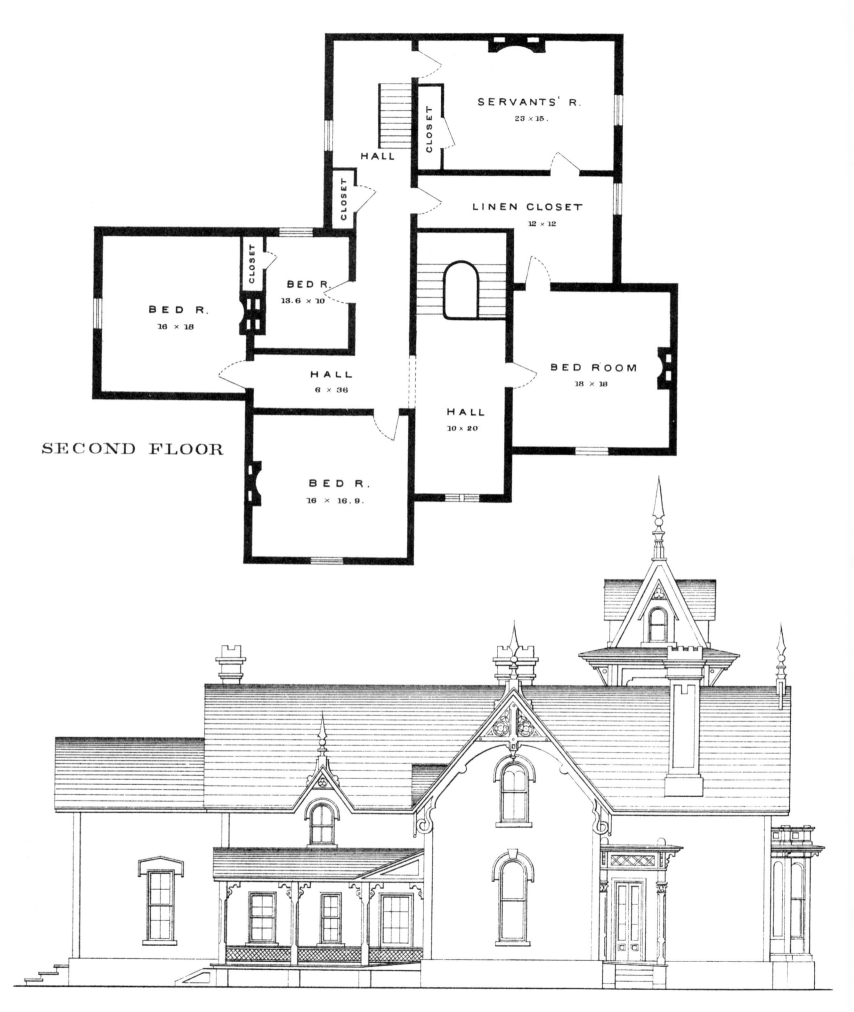

SERVANTS' R.
23 × 15.

CLOSET

HALL

LINEN CLOSET
12 × 12

CLOSET

CLOSET

BED R.
13.6 × 10

BED R.
16 × 18

BED ROOM
18 × 18

HALL
6 × 36

HALL
10 × 20

SECOND FLOOR

BED R.
16 × 16.9.

SIDE ELEVATION

PLATE 11

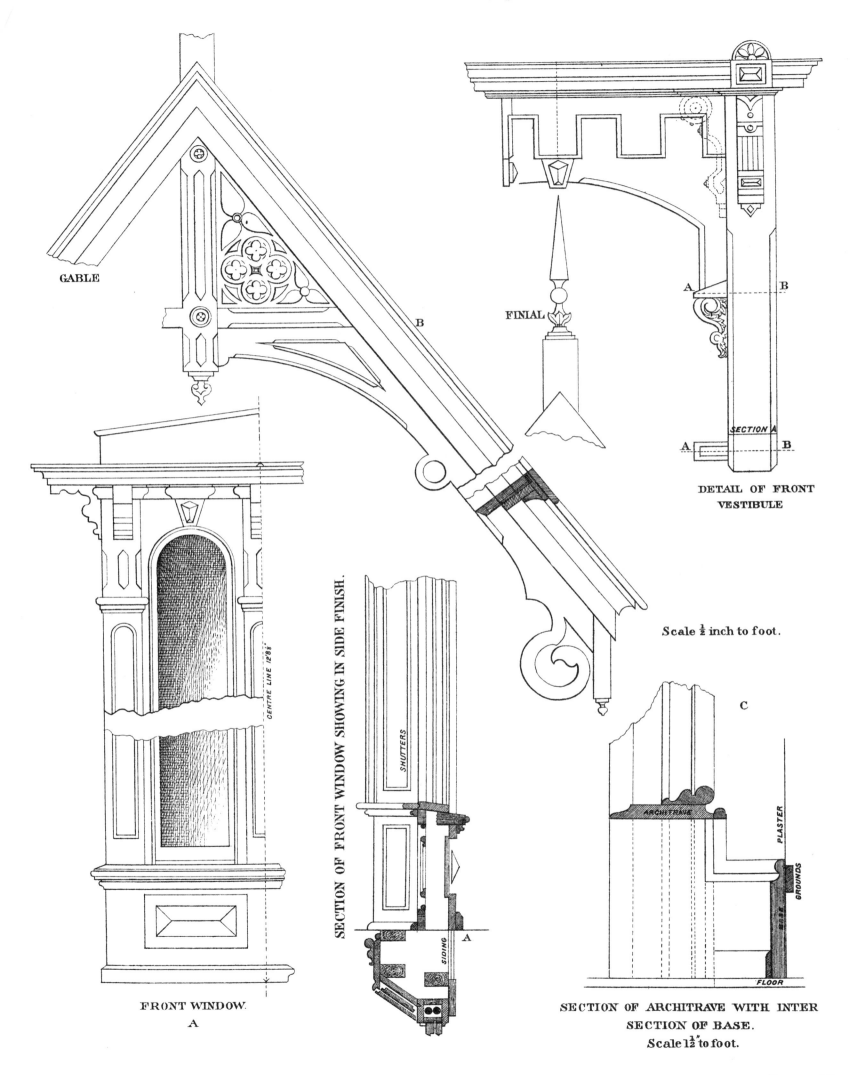

GABLE

FINIAL

DETAIL OF FRONT
VESTIBULE

SECTION A

CENTRE LINE 12'8⅛"

SECTION OF FRONT WINDOW SHOWING IN SIDE FINISH.

SHUTTERS

SIDING

A

FRONT WINDOW.

A

Scale ½ inch to foot.

C

ARCHITRAVE

PLASTER

GROUNDS

FLOOR

SECTION OF ARCHITRAVE WITH INTER
SECTION OF BASE.
Scale 1½" to foot.

PLATE 12

PLATES 13, 14.

DESIGN FOR A CHEAP RESIDENCE WITH FRENCH ROOF.

G. B. CROFF, Architect. Fort Edward, N. Y.

Plate 13. Contains the front elevation, first floor plan, and details of Cornice, Balustrade, Canopy, Window-caps, &c.

Plate 14. Shows the side elevation, plan of second floor and details for front and rear Verandah.

Scale of elevations and plans one-eighth of one inch to the foot. Details three-fourth of one inch to the foot.

This dwelling has recently been erected for John D. Bancroft, Cashier of the First National Bank of Ballston Spa, N. Y. Total cost including Architect's fees $4,000. The design presents a unique and inviting appearance and would voluntarily suggest an outlay of double the amount. The roof is covered with slate of the best quality. The frame is balloon constructed from two by four wallstrips and covered with good quality pine clap-boards, laying four inches to the weather. The first story is filled in with soft brick well laid in lime mortar. The floors are best quality Canada spruce. The exterior and interior details are of pine. The windows are hung with weights and supplied with finely finished inside blinds. The basement contains a hot-air furnace with four, nine by fourteen registers.

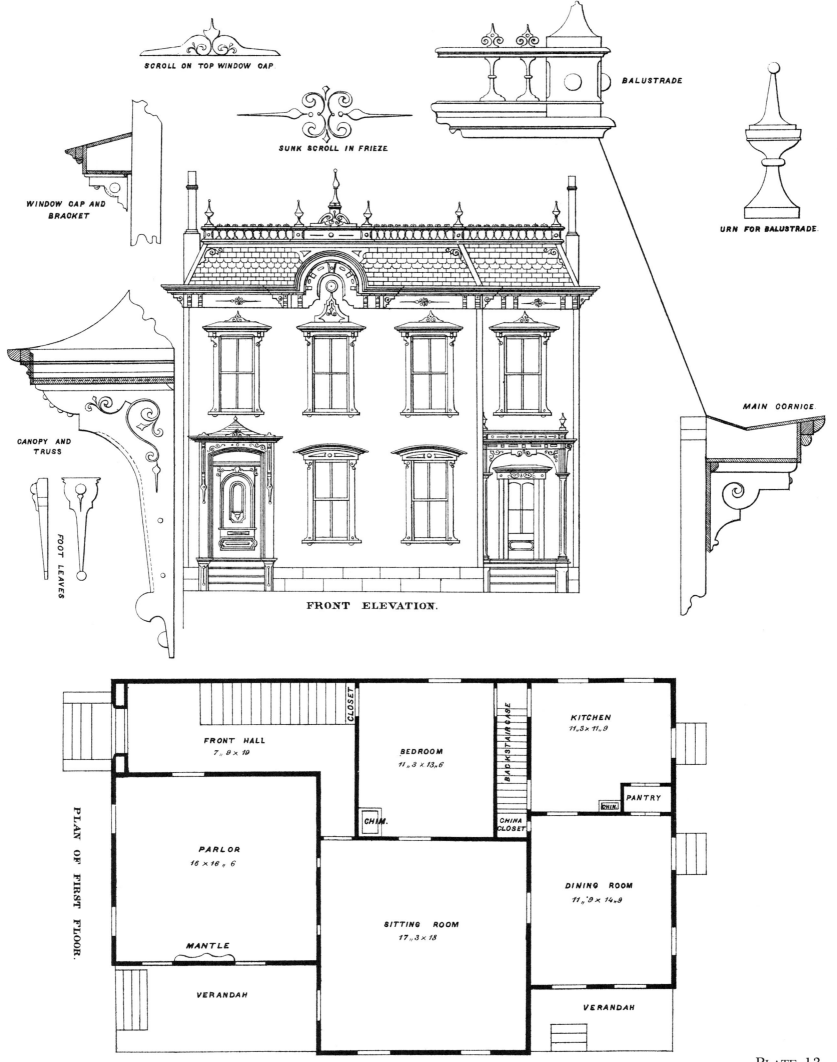

SCROLL ON TOP WINDOW CAP.

SUNK SCROLL IN FRIEZE.

BALUSTRADE

URN FOR BALUSTRADE.

WINDOW CAP AND BRACKET

CANOPY AND TRUSS

FOOT LEAVES

MAIN CORNICE.

FRONT ELEVATION.

PLAN OF FIRST FLOOR.

CLOSET

FRONT HALL
7„9 × 19

BEDROOM
11„3 × 13„6

BACKSTAIRCASE

KITCHEN
11„3 × 11„9

CHIM.

CHIN.

PANTRY

CHINA CLOSET

PARLOR
16 × 16„6

SITTING ROOM
17„3 × 18

DINING ROOM
11„9 × 14„9

MANTLE

VERANDAH

VERANDAH

PLATE 13

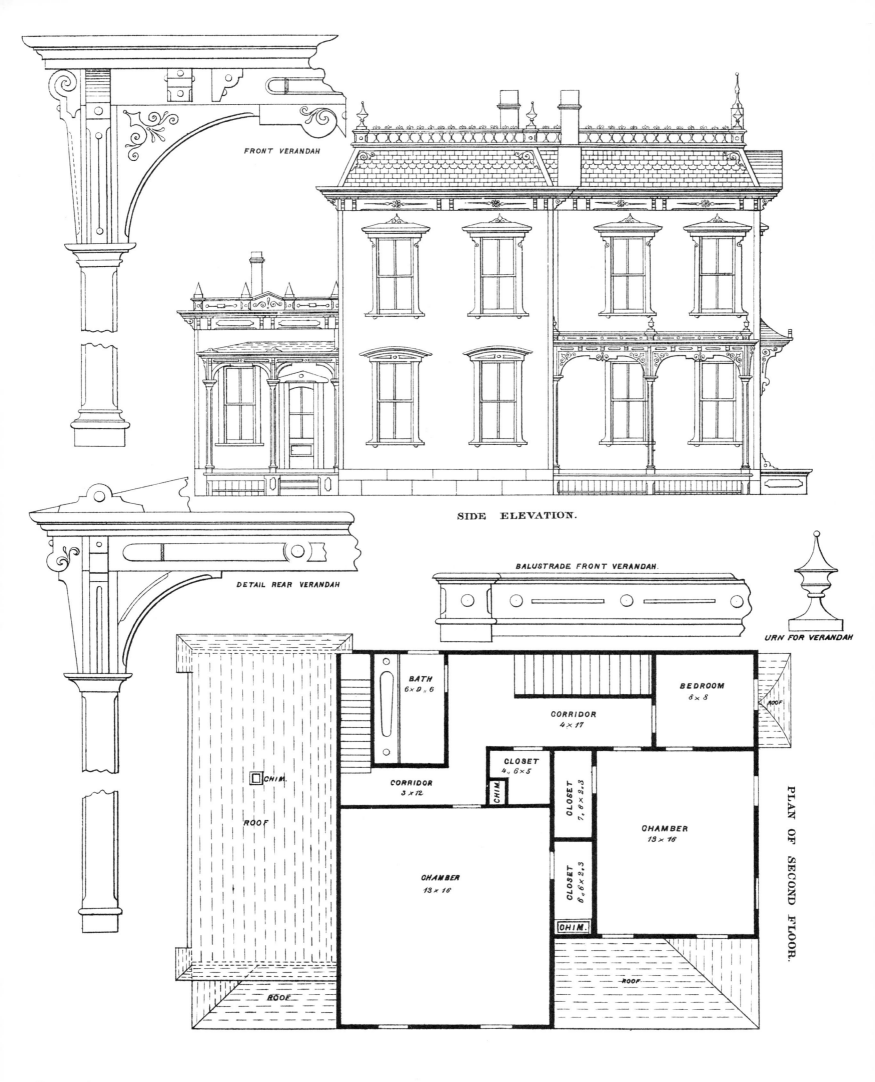

FRONT VERANDAH

SIDE ELEVATION.

DETAIL REAR VERANDAH

BALUSTRADE FRONT VERANDAH.

URN FOR VERANDAH

PLAN OF SECOND FLOOR.

BATH
6 × 9 „ 6

BEDROOM
8 × 8

ROOF

CORRIDOR
4 × 17

CHIM.

ROOF

CORRIDOR
3 × 12

CLOSET
4 „ 6 × 5

CHIM.

CLOSET
7 „ 8 × 2 „ 3

CHAMBER
13 × 16

CHAMBER
13 × 16

CLOSET
6 „ 6 × 2 „ 3

CHIM.

ROOF

ROOF

PLATE 14

PLATE 15.

DESIGN FOR A TWO STORY BRICK SUBURBAN RESIDENCE.

E. E. MYERS, Architect, Springfield, Ill.

Fig. 1. Front elevation.

Fig. 2. Side elevation.

Fig. 3. First floor plan, containing Hall, Parlor, Dining and Sitting-room, Kitchen and Pantry.

Fig. 4. Second floor, containing Guests' and Family rooms, Bath-room, two Bed-rooms and Servants' room.

Fig. 5. Basement plan. Scale sixteen feet to one inch. Cost $4,500.

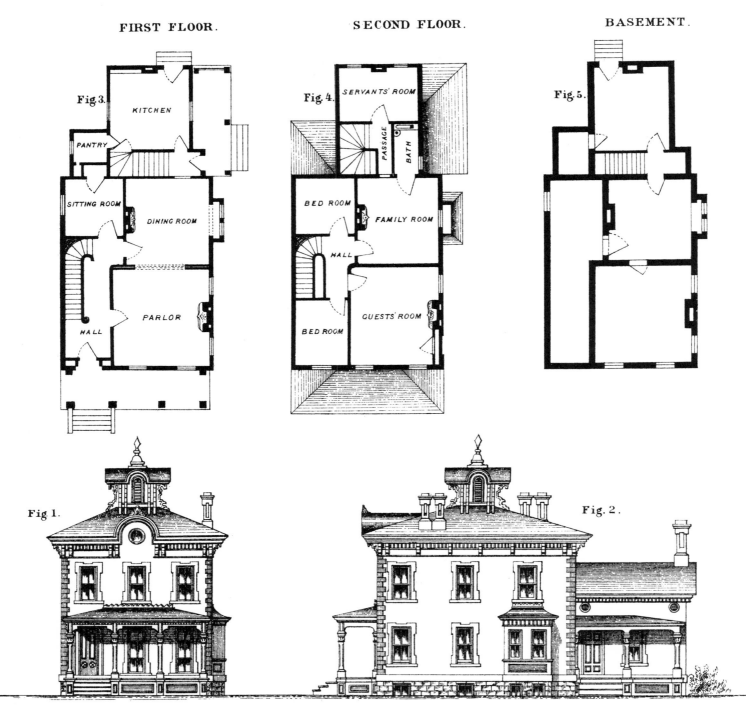

FIRST FLOOR.

SECOND FLOOR.

BASEMENT.

Fig 3.

KITCHEN

PANTRY

SITTING ROOM

DINING ROOM

PARLOR

HALL

Fig 4.

SERVANTS' ROOM

PASSAGE

BATH

BED ROOM

FAMILY ROOM

HALL

GUESTS' ROOM

BED ROOM

Fig 5.

Fig 1.

Fig. 2.

FRONT VIEW.

SIDE VIEW.

PLATE 15

PLATES 16, 17.

DESIGN FOR A DWELLING, STYLE FRENCH MANSARD.

BROWN & GRABLE, Architects, 307 Locust Street, St. Louis, Mo.

This house is suitable for a country or suburban residence. Can be built of brick or wood; cost built of merchantable brick and painted, $7,500.

Plate 16. Shows the front elevation and first story plan.

Plate 17. Plan of second story and attic.

Scale of elevation and plans eight feet to the inch.

FRONT ELEVATION

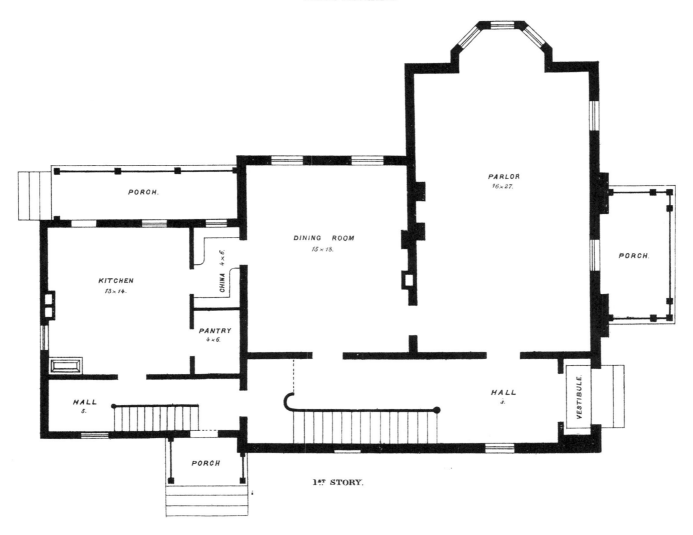

PORCH.

PARLOR
16 x 27.

DINING ROOM
15 x 18.

KITCHEN
13 x 14.

CHINA
4 x 6.

PORCH.

PANTRY
4 x 6.

HALL
5.

HALL
5.

VESTIBULE.

PORCH

1ST STORY.

PLATE 16   [plate reduced 10 per cent in this reprint edition]

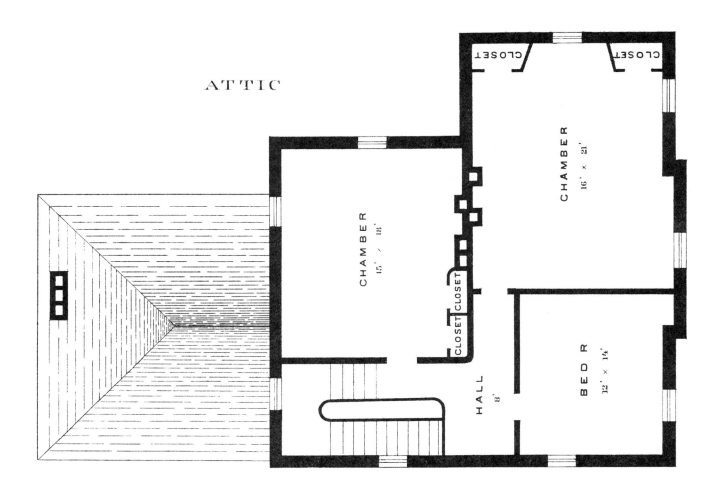

ATTIC

CHAMBER
15' × 18'

CHAMBER
16' × 21'

CLOSET

CLOSET

CLOSET

CLOSET

BED R
12' × 14'

HALL
8'

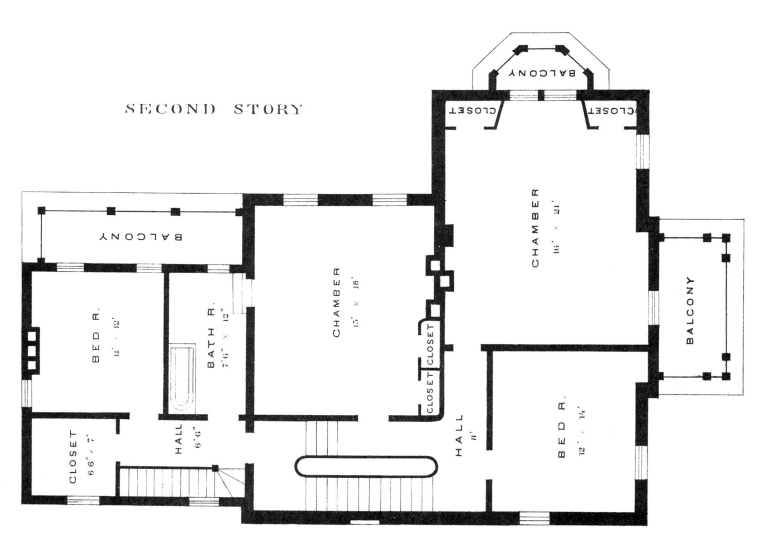

SECOND STORY

BALCONY

CHAMBER
16' × 21'

CLOSET

CLOSET

BALCONY

CHAMBER
15' × 18'

CLOSET

CLOSET

BED R.
11' × 12'

BATH R.
7'6" × 12'

BALCONY

CLOSET
6'6" × 7'

HALL
6'6"

HALL
8'

BED R.
12' × 14'

PLATE 17

PLATES 18, 19.

DESIGN OF SUBURBAN RESIDENCE.

E. E. MYERS, Architect, Springfield, Ill.

Plate 18. Front elevation and first floor plan.

Plate 19. Side elevation and second floor plan. Scale one-eighth of one inch to the foot.

This dwelling has been recently erected for W. B. Corneau, of Springfield, Ill. Cost $10,000.

FRONT ELEVATION.

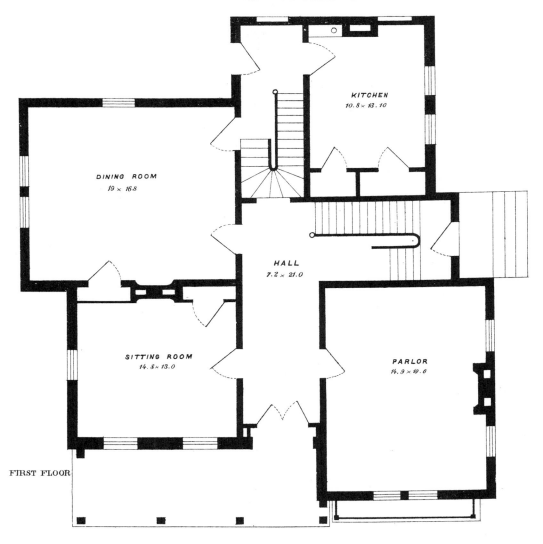

KITCHEN
10.8 × 13.10

DINING ROOM
19 × 16.8

HALL
7.2 × 21.0

SITTING ROOM
14.8 × 13.0

PARLOR
14.9 × 19.6

FIRST FLOOR

[plate reduced 10 per cent in this reprint edition]   PLATE 18

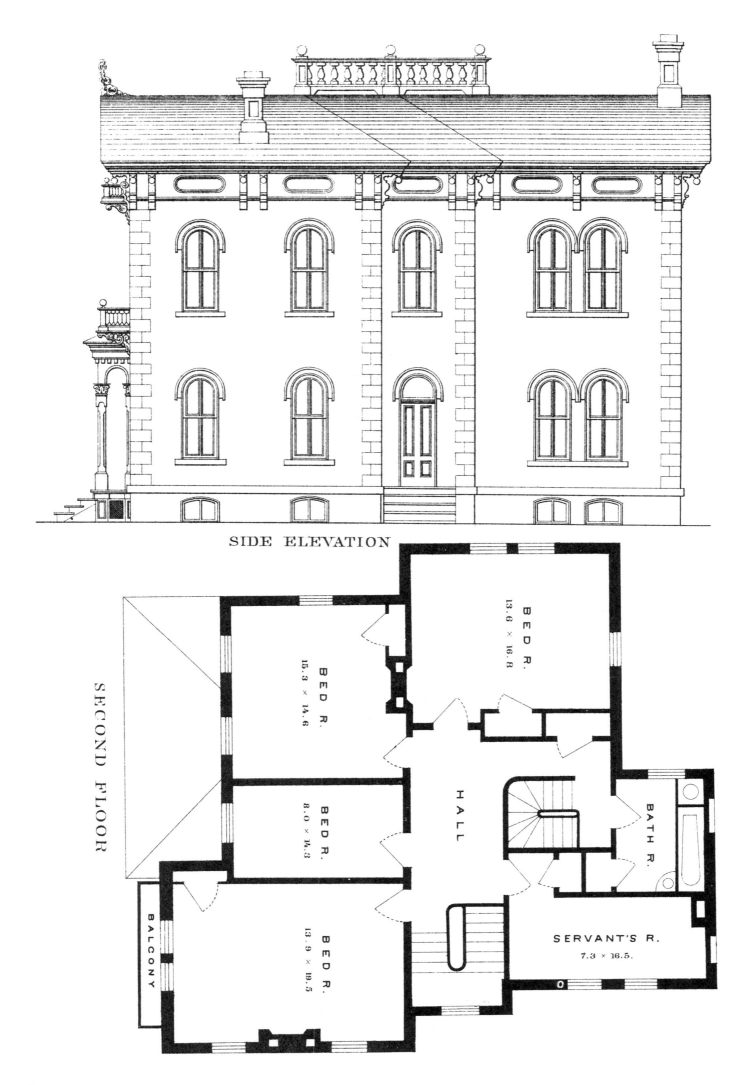

SIDE ELEVATION

SECOND FLOOR

BED R.
13.6 × 16.8

BED R.
15.3 × 14.6

BED R.
8.0 × 14.3

HALL

BATH R.

BED R.
13.9 × 19.5

BALCONY

SERVANT'S R.
7.3 × 16.5.

PLATE 19

PLATES 20, 21, 22.

DESIGN FOR A FIRST CLASS DWELLING.

E. Boydon & Son, Architects, Worcester, Mass.

Plate 20. Front elevation.

Plate 21. Rear elevation and ground plan.

Plate 22. Side elevation and chamber plan.

This house has been built for Mr. J. A. Hovey, Ballston Spa, N. Y., and is one of the best residences in that section of the country.   The cost was $30,000.

Scale of plans and elevations one inch to twelve feet.

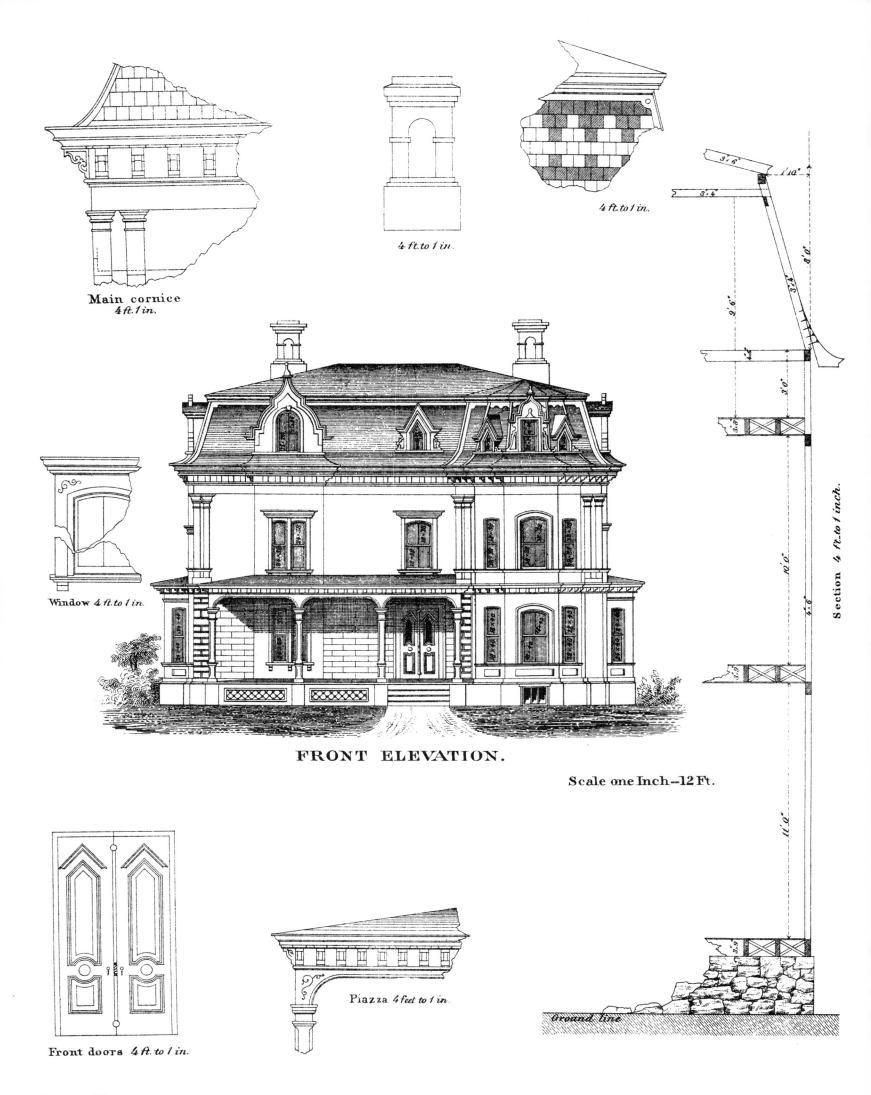

Main cornice
4 ft. 1 in.

4 ft. to 1 in.

4 ft. to 1 in.

Window 4 ft. to 1 in.

Section 4 ft. to 1 inch.

FRONT ELEVATION.

Scale one Inch—12 Ft.

Front doors 4 ft. to 1 in.

Piazza 4 feet to 1 in.

Ground line

PLATE 20

REAR ELEVATION

AND

GROUND PLAN

Scale 1-inch-12 ft.

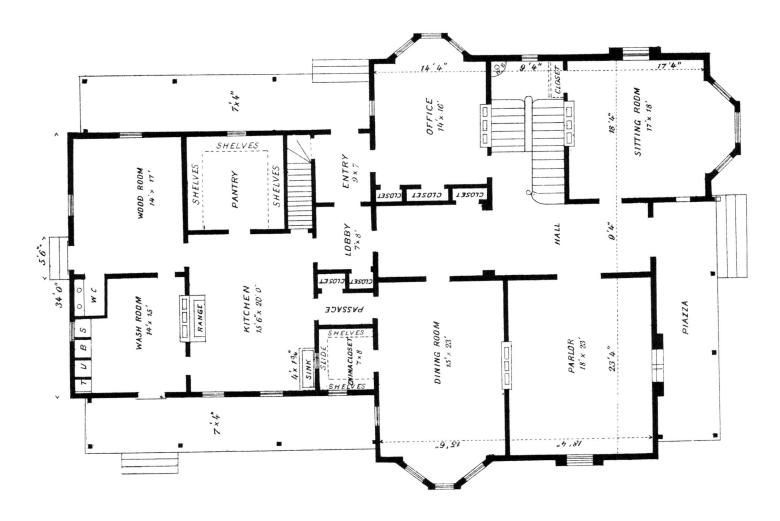

PLATE 21

FRONT VIEW

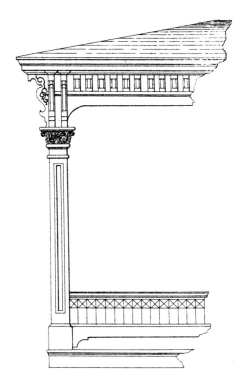

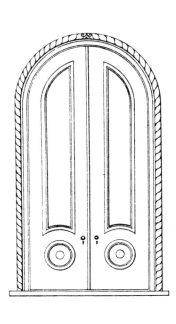

Scale of Details: ¼ of 1 inch to 1 foot.

PLATE 23

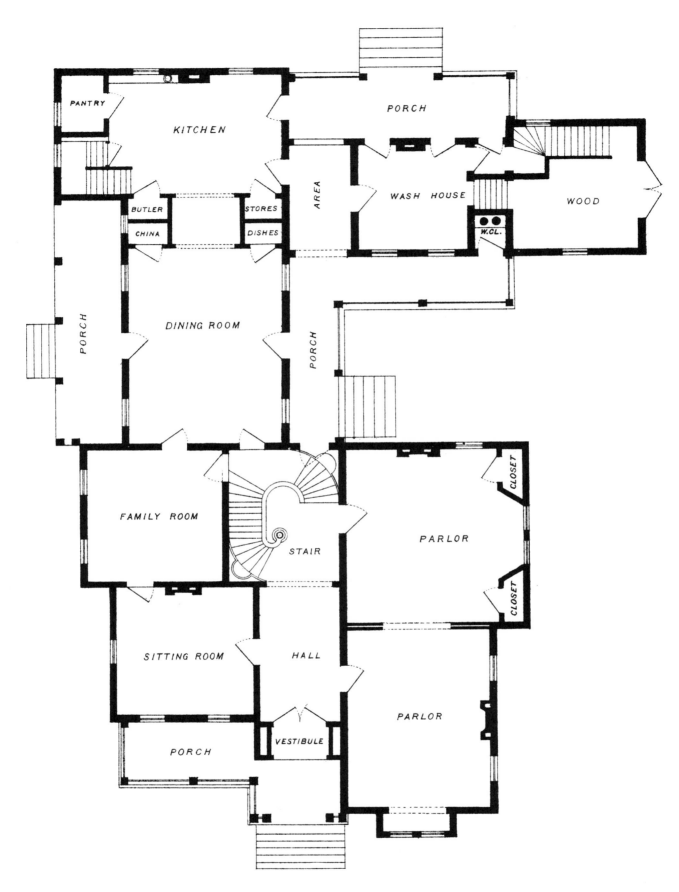

PANTRY

KITCHEN

PORCH

WASH HOUSE

WOOD

AREA

BUTLER

STORES

CHINA

DISHES

W.CL.

PORCH

DINING ROOM

PORCH

FAMILY ROOM

STAIR

PARLOR

CLOSET

CLOSET

SITTING ROOM

HALL

PARLOR

PORCH

VESTIBULE

FIRST FLOOR PLAN.

PLATE 24

SIDE VIEW.

Details ¼ of 1 inch to 1 foot.

PLATE 25

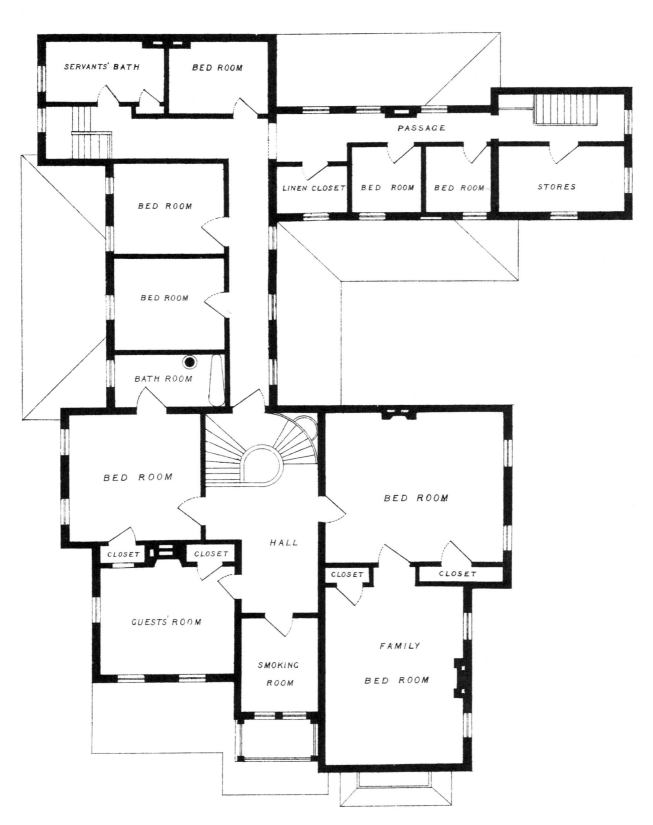

SERVANTS' BATH

BED ROOM

PASSAGE

BED ROOM

LINEN CLOSET

BED ROOM

BED ROOM

STORES

BED ROOM

BATH ROOM

BED ROOM

BED ROOM

HALL

CLOSET

CLOSET

CLOSET

CLOSET

GUESTS' ROOM

SMOKING ROOM

FAMILY BED ROOM

SECOND FLOOR.

PLATE 26

PLATES 27, 28,

DESIGN FOR A HANDSOME SUBURBAN RESIDENCE.

F. Wm. READER, Architect, 307 Locust Street, St. Louis, Mo.

Plate 27. Front elevation.

Plate 28. Plans of Basement, first floor, second floor and attic: a, denotes range; b b, dumb waiters; c c c c, wash troughs; d d, waste soil pipes; e e e e, dining-room closets; f f, flues of range and furnace; g g, hot air flues; h h, hot air registers or grates; i i i i, ventilating ducts; k k k k, chamber closets; k, hall closets; k k, closet under stairs; l l, water-closets in basement; l l l, water-closets on second floor; m m m m m, wash-stands; m, hydrant and sink.

Scale of elevation, one-eighth of one inch to the foot; scale of plan, one-sixteenth of one inch to the foot.   Cost $21,000.

FRONT ELEVATION.

Details ¼ of 1 inch to 1 foot.

PLATE 27

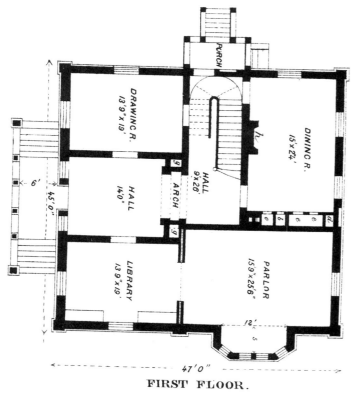

FIRST FLOOR.

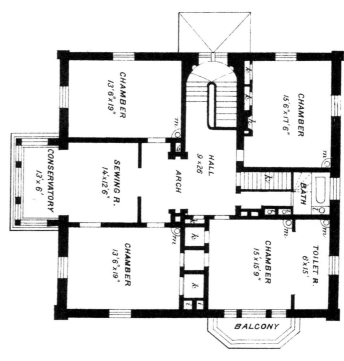

SECOND FLOOR.

BASEMENT.

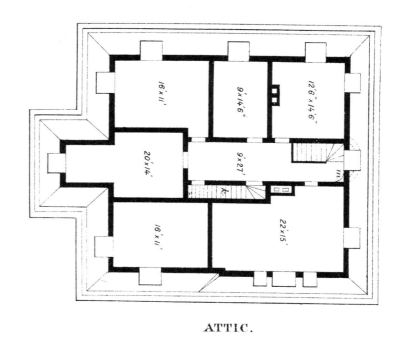

ATTIC.

PLATE 28

PLATE 29.

MODEL DESIGN FOR A CHEAP CITY DWELLING.

C. Bolin Stark, Architect, Philadelphia, Pa.

This Plate shows the front elevation, section and plans of a city residence of moderate cost. The basement has a kitchen, closet, and coal cellar; the first story ante-room, dining-room and closets; the second story contains library and parlor; third story—bed-room, dressing-room, bath-room and closet.

Scale—one-eighth of one inch to the foot. Cost, built of brick and plainly furnished, $2,000

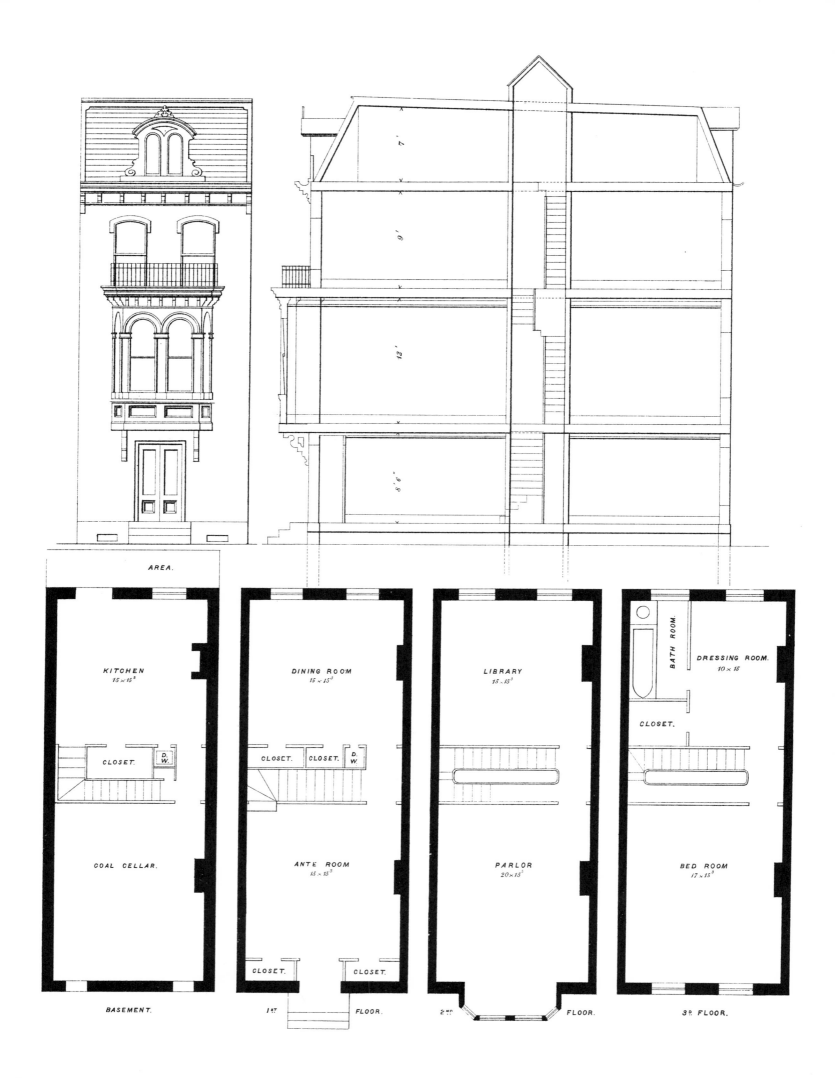

AREA.

KITCHEN
15 × 15⁸

CLOSET. D. W.

COAL CELLAR.

BASEMENT.

DINING ROOM
15 × 15⁹

CLOSET. CLOSET. D. W.

ANTE ROOM
15 × 15⁹

CLOSET. CLOSET.

1ˢᵗ   FLOOR.

LIBRARY
15 × 15⁹

PARLOR
20 × 15⁹

2ᴺᴰ   FLOOR.

BATH ROOM. DRESSING ROOM.
10 × 15

CLOSET.

BED ROOM
17 × 15⁹

3ᴰ. FLOOR.

PLATE 29   [plate reduced 10 per cent in this reprint edition]

PLATES 30, 31.

PERSPECTIVE VIEW, FRONT ELEVATION AND PLAN FOR A FIRST-CLASS STABLE.

E. BOYDEN & SON, Architects, Worcester, Mass.

This stable has been recently erected for a gentleman at Worcester, Mass. The style of his residence is Elizabethan, and the stable is made to correspond. Cost $5,000.

PLATE 30